A Peck of Salt

A Peck of Salt

A Year in the Ghetto

BY

JOHN T. HOUGH, Jr.

An Atlantic Monthly Press Book

Boston   Little, Brown and Company   *Toronto*

ATLANTIC–LITTLE, BROWN BOOKS
ARE PUBLISHED BY
LITTLE, BROWN AND COMPANY
IN ASSOCIATION WITH
THE ATLANTIC MONTHLY PRESS

Published simultaneously in Canada
by Little, Brown & Company (Canada) Limited

PRINTED IN THE UNITED STATES OF AMERICA

*To Ronald Wiggens
and David Walton*

It is a true saying, that a man must eat a peck of salt with his friend, before he knows him.

—CERVANTES

I

Nowhere Without a Brother

ONE

I THOUGHT, that spring of 1968, that I was going to make a good Vista volunteer. I had played high school and small college football, traveled to Europe, and worked as a newspaper reporter. I had never had to quit anything I had started. I felt equipped to invade the world of urban poverty, stark and menacing as that world seemed.

I grew up on Cape Cod, in the small town of Falmouth, where my father published a newspaper. I went to high school there and was graduated in English literature from Haverford College. I was twenty-two. I had never seen an inner city.

Spring came early, and summer was full-blown in June. The dry brown hills of Martha's Vineyard, visible across the sound on a clear day, were suddenly hazed with long grass and blueberry bushes. The decks of the ferry fluttered with shirtsleeves and bell-bottom slacks. The water was emerald-blue. And Bobby Kennedy was murdered. They had got Martin Luther King in April, now they got Bobby. The swimmers and sailboats were out as usual, but all day the radios crackled medical reports. He died. It was dangerous out there.

My parents approved of my going into Vista. They thought the country could be saved by the determined, idealistic young. They had brought me up to believe the same. My brother and three sisters, all younger than I, had already decided they were going to follow me into Vista.

I went to bed early the night before I left home. The grass had been cut. I could still smell its sweet juices. A moth bounced off the screen. My suitcase sat packed and open on the floor, waiting for a shirt my mother would iron in the morning. I felt the way I had the night before I first left home for college, but the sensation was sharper now. There was a huge framed print by Frederic Remington hanging above the mantel. It had hung in my father's room years ago, and it had always been the last thing I saw before I turned out the light. It showed a half-breed kneeling on a tawny knoll, his rifle across his knee. Indians on horses circled at the bottom of the hill. The rugged brown half-breed squinted out at me. He had been up there, studying me, for a long time now.

Next morning I boarded a jet plane in Boston and left a world behind.

Forty Vista volunteers came to Chicago that first day of August. We were put in the YMCA on Wabash Avenue. We would live there until Vista sent us to live and work in the slums. "We have taken training out of the classroom and moved it to the neighborhoods," they told us at the first lecture. We would work at community agencies. We would be supervised. The training period would last six weeks, and then we would be assigned to projects all over the Great Lakes region. Only a few of us would stay in Chicago.

I got my first lesson about the black ghetto the day after I arrived.

It was a hot, humid morning, the sunlight white and dazzling. There was nothing to do, and a volunteer named Randy suggested to me at breakfast in the YMCA cafeteria that we see the University of Chicago. It sounded like a good idea. We checked our maps and discovered that we had to take the Chicago Transit Authority bus south on State Street, and walk from State Street to the university. Neither of us had ever heard of the South Side of Chicago.

Randy was a pale blond kid with long curly hair. He had finished a year at Harvard and decided to take a year off.

We got off the bus somewhere near Sixtieth Street, deep in the South Side, and walked east. The sidewalks were jammed. Old men and women dragged their feet, and young foreheads sweated. Cheap eating places, dry cleaners, and dingy grocery stores lined the sidewalk in the hot shadows of the el tracks. In every window, it seemed, was a photograph of Martin Luther King.

All of the hundreds of people who crowded the streets and sidewalks and doorways were black. I had never seen so many black people. I kept wondering what they thought of us. I tried to look nonchalant.

It took us more than an hour to find the university. We wandered up and down side streets beside blackened brick walls and deserted tenement buildings. Soul music throbbed from dark doorways. I saw for the first time the messages scrawled in chalk and paint: *Black Power . . . Devil's Disciples . . . Ann is a hoe she kiss my ass.*

The university was like an island among the filthy, littered streets. Its buildings had flat roofs and glass walls, and waxed floors. Generous swirls from sprinklers swept the lawns. Randy and I walked in and out of the buildings. There were a few students around, and occasional professors with briefcases. Late in the afternoon we started back to State Street.

That was when we got into trouble. We were walking west on a quiet, narrow street. Three-story tenement buildings pushed to the edge of the sidewalk. Children sat on the porches; old women leaned out of windows and fanned themselves with folded newspapers. Two blocks from State Street we passed a crowded porch and I caught sight of a young black face at a ground-floor window.

"Whitey!"

It was a long, shrill hiss, and I think it came from the face at the window. Other voices picked it up. "Whitey! Whitey!" The shouts chased us, laced with hoots and cackles. We kept walking. I'd never been so scared.

What did they have against me? It was crazy. I had come to this city to help children like these, maybe to help these very children.

A beer can clattered past our feet. A bottle smashed on the pavement behind us and another beer can bounced off my calf. We walked faster. One more bottle splashed around our ankles. The cries dissolved. I glanced back. Several of them were following us at a distance on bicycles.

We got to State Street. Cars hurtled past, the sun glinting on their chrome. I peered into the distance for a bus.

At the corner, three teen-agers straddling bicycles studied us like meditative cowboys. One by one they took off, riding in circles. They sheered closer to us with every turn. They had impassive faces and slick straightened hair. Finally one rammed Randy. Randy grabbed the bike by the handlebar and the kid spat in his face and spun away.

A bus swerved to the curb. We scrambled up the steps, and before the driver could close the door, a rock the size of a softball bounced at our feet. The black driver shook his head and watched us drop our coins into the box. My legs felt soft as I shuffled down the aisle. The bus was filled with middle-aged black people. They stared past us sullenly, as though they had problems of their own.

I dropped into a seat. My face and back were dripping. "Jesus," I whispered.

Randy glanced at me. "What would have happened?"

"I don't know."

"Maybe we should have told them we're in Vista," Randy said.

"You know something?" I said. "It wouldn't have made any difference. Not even if we explained what Vista is." I was scared.

I was one of four Vista volunteers assigned to the Mile Square Federation, a community organization of the people in a carefully measured square mile on the West Side. Two of us were black, the only black volunteers in the training group.

Brett was twenty-five, older than anyone else by plenty. He told us he had worked for SNCC and CORE, and he said he had seen a policeman break his brother's jaw with the heel of a revolver in a jail in San Francisco. He also said he had been in Vista before. He was lean and finely sculptured, with sideburns and a mustache. The other black kid was only nineteen. His name was Wesley. He had finished two years of college and was drifting.

Then there was Stanley Hastings. Stanley had read all of Faulkner and played junior varsity basketball at Rutgers. He had dark eyebrows that arched way up and made him look like a grinning cartoon character, no matter what his mouth was doing.

It rained the morning the four of us left the Y. We drove along Wabash to Madison Street, turned west, and followed Madison all the way to the Mile Square Federation. The rain petered out and a gray ceiling hung low. Madison Street looked greasy. The Mile Square Federation stood wedged between a dry cleaner's and a small grocery store.

We walked in. It was an old storefront, a long, low room with plywood walls splashed with pale green paint. It had three battered wooden desks, a pair of filing cabinets, and a tangle of folding chairs and old wooden school desks. Flies looped below the fluorescent tubes close to the smudged ceiling. A short, stocky man with a goatee was sitting on top of a desk.

"I'm you all's trainer," he said. "Virgil Bateman."

Virgil had just become president of the Mile Square Federation, and Vista didn't know much about him. It turned out he was a big hustler. He drove an air-conditioned Buick and lived in a luxurious apartment outside the ghetto. Three blocks from the Mile Square Federation stood Virgil's pool hall, a narrow, dark, dirty little room where deals were made across pool tables. At any time of day you could see two or three Cadillacs parked in front of the door. Huge rings and cufflinks flashed in the cigarette smoke above the green felt tables, while men with coiffured hair held council in corners. Vista didn't know about the pool hall. I don't know where Virgil expected the presidency to fit in with his career, but it must not have, for he resigned before our training period ended. I saw him in the office three times in six weeks.

But that first morning he was waiting for us. He sat on one of the metal chairs, his arms folded on its back. He was a very neat man with creased slacks and polished shoes. We all shook hands with him.

"And this here's Bobby Brassfield," he said, jerking his head at a kid who leaned against the wall. Bobby was very dark and was built like a professional halfback. He wore a dungaree jacket over a T-shirt and squinted through thick glasses.

"Sit down," Virgil said. We pulled folding chairs into a semicircle. "Now I'm gonna be honest with you," he said. "The Federation is a joke. It ain't been doin nothin and it ain't doin nothin now. Except for me, the officers is all old people who ain't got no idea what's goin on with the young brothers in the streets."

Brett studied Virgil and nodded slowly. A few hours earlier in the Y cafeteria Brett had been telling me about the 1967 riot in Watts. I felt like a new recruit sent suddenly to the front. Wesley, the other black kid, glanced sideways at Brett, the veteran, and nodded when he did. Wesley had grown up in a pleasant neighborhood outside Pittsburgh. Stanley sat still, his eyebrows arched in that cartoon grimace.

"There ain't no organization," Virgil went on. "Everybody fightin among themselves. The Federation supposed to be checkin housin complaints, giving legal aid, organizin tenants. Only one doin anythin is Brass, here." He jerked his head at Bobby. Bobby was leaning against a filing cabinet, his right knee jauntily bent.

Virgil glanced at his watch. "So you all see what you can do."

He examined Stanley and me for a moment and smiled. It was a merry smile above the fuzzy goatee. "I don't know how you boys gonna make out," he said. "I told 'em not to send me no white boys." I stared at the scraped cement floor. "It just ain't a good idea, you know? There's a war goin on, and they send the enemy to help us." Brett laughed, and then Wesley laughed too. I glanced at Stanley. His expression didn't change. Maybe he thought Virgil was kidding. Virgil continued. "Only thing I got to say is be careful. Don't go nowhere without a brother. And don't never go into the projects without one. I don't want you to lose an eye or get your brains knocked out."

Lose an eye? What was wrong with the people in cities?

"I got to pull up," Virgil said. "I'll see you all." The clouds were scattering and the sunlight plunged through the gaps onto Madison Street. We said good-bye to Bobby and drove to the house where we were to spend the next six weeks.

It was a shingled house on Washington Boulevard on what Virgil called the nicest block in the neighborhood. An old black couple named Turner met us on the porch. They were wrinkled and brown and had kind smiles. Their children had grown up and gone, and the Turners needed company. Virgil had said old people like the

Turners didn't know what was happening in the streets. Mr. Turner led us upstairs to a suite of two rooms. Brett walked into the bigger room, the one next to the bathroom, and slung his suitcase onto a bed. Wesley followed him and claimed the other bed the same way. Mr. Turner was in the bathroom checking the water. I watched Brett open his suitcase. He lifted out a folded white shirt as though it were alive and sleeping. I shrugged and took a bed in the smaller room. There really wasn't much difference between the two rooms, and just then I wanted Brett on my side.

Next morning Bobby Brassfield took Stanley and me on a tour of the neighborhood. Brett and Wesley didn't come. I don't know where they were. I assumed Brett didn't need a close inspection of a ghetto anyway.

The temperature was ninety-two. Stanley and I met Bobby in the office. It was shady and still cool in there, and Bobby sat with his feet on a desk and grinned at us as we came in.

"What's happenin?" he said.

He was wearing his dungaree jacket and a T-shirt, blue jeans and sneakers. "You ready?" He sounded like a guide who liked us so much he was going to show us the Forum and the Colosseum free.

We followed him out of the office, back across Madison, and along Leavitt Street to the Medical Center on Washington Boulevard. "You gonna see the nicest part first," Bobby told us. He walked fast, bent forward, his

shoulders bobbing. Washington Boulevard was where
the Turners lived. The trees cast huge damp shadows.
There were shingled houses and apartment buildings
that had once been elegant homes. Several young black
men in white medical outfits sat in the shade on the steps
to the medical center. They grinned at Bobby. "What's
happenin, man?" they said.

It was a four-story hospital. It was financed by the
Office of Economic Opportunity, and later I heard Virgil say it was a good thing. It was staffed by members of
the community and by outsiders, and I saw plenty of
white people. It was air-conditioned and full of fresh
linen and chilled drinking fountains. I wanted to get out
and see the ghetto. Every time Bobby took us into a new
room and introduced us to someone, Stanley would ask
some complicated question. The interns and nurses were
delighted, and they gave careful explanations and sometimes pulled out charts. The shadows had shrunk and
the temperature had risen by the time we got outside.

Bobby led us across an empty lot on Leavitt, past St.
Andrew's Church. Bobby made his living as sexton at
St. Andrew's. It was a little stone building that seemed
about to pitch forward into Leavitt Street.

We turned on Madison and headed west. We passed
hot dog stands, barrooms, laundromats, food stores.
There were neon signs in windows and on roofs, and
every letter seemed to be crooked and every sign seemed
to be painted yellow. The only interruptions in the solid
line of storefronts were the cindery empty lots.

Bobby waved at one more than fifty yards long. "This here was a furniture store," he said. "Right next to it was a grocery store." They had been burned after the King assassination. In some places the charred brick walls still stood. They were filled with whiskey bottles and garbage. You could smell it in the wicked heat. "See that one?" Bobby pointed. "That cat was selling us rotten fruit and low-grade meat. We tried to complain to the Board of Health, but didn't nothin work."

"How do they do it?" I asked. "Burn the buildings, I mean." I was trying to imagine the flames.

"They throw gas bombs," Bobby said. "What you all call a Molotov cocktail. You take a bottle, fill it with gas, and stuff some cotton or rags into the neck."

We turned south on Western Avenue. The Mile Square Federation was supposed to serve everyone within a square mile, and we were walking the perimeter. Western looked like Madison, but it was wider and busier. Across Western, outside the Mile Square, rose the new Rockwell Housing Project. It was made of brick and looked like a hospital. On the asphalt playground surrounding the project kids were playing baseball and dodgeball. I don't know how they did it in that heat.

"Along the street here the gangs from Rockwell and the gangs from the Horner Project snipe at each other," Bobby said.

Snipe at each other?

We turned east on Jackson Boulevard. There were houses on Jackson, shoulder to shoulder along torn and crumbling sidewalks. Windows were broken, porches sagged. Every house was dark inside. Madison and Western, in spite of the cheapness and grime, looked tough and regenerative. Jackson Boulevard seemed to have given up.

A clot of kids studied us from a porch. "Don't you come walking here without me," Bobby said. The kids watched us. "Sometimes somebody be in a bad mood, they gonna jump on you."

Bobby pointed to a huge empty lot to our right, between us and the Congress Expressway. "That's where they gonna build the next project," he said. "We don't want it, but the city don't care nothin about that. We gonna go see the Horner Project now."

We walked along Ashland Avenue, the third boundary of the Mile Square. Ashland was as wide as Western, but a mile closer to downtown and more affluent. There were some insurance offices, the office of one of the local unions, and a YMCA. White people speckled the crowds on the sidewalk.

The Horner Project was on Lake Street. It was a complex of three brick monoliths, like the blocks of child-giants dropped on the asphalt. Boys and girls were playing with an old softball. Its stitches were torn and a piece of the hide cover flapped loose. Some of the children waved to Bobby.

"Black concentration camps," he said. "We want to buy homes, not live stacked on top of each other."

We walked along Lake Street, under the el tracks.

The tracks made shade, and it was a little like being in a tunnel. Washington Boulevard was a block away, and the tour was almost ended. Even in the shadow of the el tracks it was scorching, and my shirt squeezed my wet back. Suddenly the rails overhead began to vibrate. There was a rumble, like thunder in the distance, and then the el blasted by, screeching and roaring so that you couldn't hear yourself shout. The last car flicked past, and the howl faded and died. We took Leavitt Street back to the office, the echo of the el still ringing in our ears.

Bobby and I answered a housing complaint the next day. It was the first of dozens of calls we made together that summer. The morning was gray and humid, but nearly as hot as usual. Stanley sat at a desk at the front of the office studying a clutter of papers and file cards. He had put a sign in the window that said APPLY FOR JOBS HERE, and he was telephoning businessmen in the community and asking them to hire the kids that came into the office. He talked to the kids and the businessmen as though he had been a personnel manager all his life. Brett and Wesley were out as usual.

The door swung open and a man and woman and their child shuffled in.

"Can I help you?" Bobby called from the back of the room. He was sitting at the desk there. He tossed a pen at me. "You gonna be my secretary," he said. I flipped open a pad and dragged up a chair.

"We want to make a housing complaint," the man said. He wore a black jersey and had a long face with bristling gray whiskers. The woman was fat and shapeless. Her cotton dress was frayed and faded. They must have been close to fifty.

"Sit down," Bobby said. He looked very serious in his glasses. The couple sat on folding chairs in front of the desk. The little girl squirmed on her mother's lap.

"What's your name?" Bobby asked. They glanced at each other. "We ain't gonna tell no one," Bobby said.

"Matthews," the man said. I wrote it.

"We got rats and roaches," the woman said. "I ain't got no place to store nothin and the . . ."

"You hush up," her husband snapped. "He gonna ask you when he want you to speak." He smiled at Bobby. "She get excited, you know how it is."

"Where do you live?" Bobby asked.

"On West Jackson." I wrote it.

"What's the landlord's name and address?"

Mr. and Mrs. Matthews sought help in each other's eyes. "I don't know where he live," Mr. Matthews said. "He just come and take the rent and go away."

"His name Mr. Burch," Mrs. Matthews said.

"You don't know his first name?"

"He just come and get his money."

"Can we see the building?" Bobby asked.

"You sure can."

They got up. Bobby drew a mimeographed sheet

17

from the filing cabinet and gave it to me. Stanley was talking on the phone.

"Come on, man," Bobby said.

Mr. and Mrs. Matthews walked very slowly. The child tottered at their side. They walked as if they had no particular place to go and nothing in the world to do. The little girl gazed with huge, wondering eyes. Her legs were bare; she wore a filthy red smock.

"How long you been livin there?" Bobby asked.

"Nine months. We want to move, but we can't find no place."

We headed south on Winchester Street, past sooty tenement buildings. Years ago, these had been handsome brick houses. You could imagine them as they had been, with elm trees beside the front walks and piano music floating out of open windows. Now, five or six families lived in each building.

We crossed Adams Street and turned east on Jackson Boulevard.

"We pay eighty-seven dollars a month," Mrs. Matthews said.

She led us through a black gaping doorway into an unlighted hall. Mr. Matthews started up the stairs. The hall smelled of beer and urine. The walls were cracked. There was a cardboard sign tacked to the wall at the landing: NO LOITERING IN HALLWAYS. CHILDREN ARE NOT TO PLAY ON THE STAIRS — J. A. BURCH, MGR.

We trudged along a stinking hall. "Community bath-room," Mrs. Matthews said, waving at a room with no door. The bathtub stood above the floor on ornate legs. The room looked like the bathroom in a basement somewhere that hasn't been used for years.

Mr. Matthews stopped at a battered door and shoved the key into the lock. His face looked old and blue in the dark hall. We walked in.

The kitchen looked like a storeroom. It was about five by seven yards. Tin cans, paper bags, cardboard boxes covered the table and spilled all over the floor. A white tin locker stood against the wall as though held at bay by the stuff at its feet. The walls were peeling, the window casing rotten. There was a sink, like a bath-room sink, and a little refrigerator. Mrs. Matthews pulled open the locker door, and the cockroaches scattered across a carton of oatmeal.

We peered into the next room. A double bed and a crib filled it. The walls were the color of black raspberry ice cream.

"Is that it?" Bobby asked.

"That's it."

"This is the whole apartment?" I asked.

"Sure is."

"You pay eighty-seven dollars for this?" I asked.

"Yes, sir."

"All right," Bobby said to me. "Fill out that form." The mimeographed sheet had lines for the name and ad-

dress of tenant and landlord and a list of possible viola-
tions. Bobby ticked them off, and I checked them. I had
to check almost every one.

"We sure do thank you all for comin around," Mr.
Matthews said.

"We'll call the landlord," Bobby said. "If he don't do
nothin, we'll call the city."

We clattered down the steps and out onto the sidewalk along Jackson. We went to a lot of homes that
summer, and all were about the same as the Matthews's
apartment. Some were bigger, but these held so many
more people that the size didn't matter.

"Will the landlord do anything about it?" I asked.

"Nope."

"Will the city?"

"Man, who knows?"

"Do they ever?"

"Sometimes."

They knew Bobby Brassfield all over the neighborhood. The children playing ball and hopscotch by the
projects would wave and yell as we walked past. Mr.
and Mrs. Turner knew him, and so did the white people
who owned the stores up and down Madison Street. But
better than anyone else, the gangs from the projects
knew him.

I saw these kids, usually in the early evening, on
street corners or hanging around near the doors to the
projects. They were lean and loose and they stared icily

at me. They wore bright slacks — green was the favorite color — and they were very clean. Some had processed hair. They drank beer out of cans wrapped in paper bags and smoked cigarettes. "What's happenin?" they said, and Bobby jerked his fist upward, the black power salute.

Bobby had run with the gangs since he was eleven. He had stolen, sold marijuana, whored, and fought with the boys from across Western Avenue. He was twenty, and he didn't have a police record. Now to live that long on the West Side without getting picked up by the police takes plenty of intelligence. Bobby had it, and a good pair of legs.

A year ago, he told me, he had left the gangs. He left them for a girl. Her name was Pat. She was an American Indian, a bronze girl with silken hair. She lived with Bobby in a two-room apartment on Washington Boulevard, five doors from the Turners' house. Pat was pregnant. Bobby had taken the job as sexton at St. Andrew's to feed Pat and pay the rent. His work at the Mile Square Federation was volunteer.

Although Bobby was two years younger than I, I thought of him as the older. He called me "son" and "junior" and took me anywhere I wanted to go. He showed me parts of the ghetto I never could have seen alone. We went out almost every night after dinner. Stanley came once in a while. Brett and Wesley never came.

Until the evenings got cool we went to the public

swimming pool at the edge of Union Park. Bobby had worked there two summers as lifeguard. The sun would be dropping behind the rooftops and the pool would be chilly and dark. It was choked with kids. We changed into our bathing suits in the locker room. Outside I felt naked and frail among so many black, sinewy bodies. Bobby played in the water like a rambunctious fish. He was full of sudden energies and he leaped at friends and shoved their heads under. Some of them battled back, some told him to quit playing. The lifeguard was a good friend of Bobby's. He was very pleasant to me. I swam up and down carefully, afraid even to bump someone by accident. I felt delicate and defenseless and at the same time obtrusive. A bare light bulb was burning in the locker room when the pool closed. We would dress, say good-bye to the lifeguard, and walk across Union Park and down Washington Boulevard in the thickening dusk. I felt exhilarated — not from the swim, but from having been the only white person in the pool. Of course I could not have been there without Bobby.

The swimming pool had been built by the City of Chicago. When the heat gets unbearable, the kids take off their shirts and sneakers and collect at the fire hydrants. Someone opens the hydrant with a wrench, and they wrap an inner tube around its trunk. The water rushes against the tube and is sent fifteen feet into the air. The kids scamper in and out of their street-corner fountain. They wallow in the torrent that sluices along the gutter.

On a July day three years ago, two policemen had parked their cruiser next to an open hydrant, pushed through the bathers, and clamped on the lid. The gutter emptied. The kids backed off, glowering at the cops. Someone threw a brick at the police car. The crowd was getting bigger, and another brick splintered the cruiser's windshield. The cops radioed for help. The battle spread, and Chicago's first major riot swept the West and South Sides.

It lasted three days. By the end of the summer, the city had built the swimming pool.

"Violence," Virgil Bateman said, holding his palms out like an Italian. "You tell me violence is wrong. But violence was the only way we was gonna get that swimmin pool. And you ain't gonna tell me those kids don't need a pool."

One night Bobby took me to the Imperial Movie Theater on Madison Street near Western Avenue. We went with Louis, a piano player who headed a trio that made good money playing at night spots in the neighborhood. I had met Louis in the office. He helped us when he had time.

The streetlights and neon signs were blinking on as we walked down Madison Street. Bobby and Louis flanked me like bodyguards. Three kids on a corner called to Louis, and he stopped and chatted with them in low tones. As we walked on, Louis told me, "That small dude is some boxer. He can really thump." We walked into the lobby of the theater without stopping at the ticket window. Two kids were standing at the door in the lobby. One was wearing a lime-colored suit, the other wore blue jeans and a T-shirt. Bobby introduced them to me and they shook my hand.

"How come you don't have to pay?" I asked Bobby as we walked into the dark auditorium.

"Man, we own this neighborhood," Bobby said.

The movie was an English thriller called *The Phantom of Soho*. The murderer turned out to be a woman newspaper reporter. The theater was half full. There were teen-agers and their girls, clutches of little boys, and some solitary old men. Bobby and Louis talked out loud and made salacious remarks about the women.

Madison Street was lighted up when we came out of the theater. Pink and blue neon signs glowed voluptuously. James Brown screeched in stereo from an open record shop, while two girls writhed in a soulful dance in the lighted doorway. Several men leaned against a parked car, studying them and sipping beer. On the corner a group of men passed around a bottle. One of them was saying, "If that motherfucker fuck with my girl again, I'll kill him. No jive, I'll kill him."

We left Madison Street, and Bobby and Louis watched me climb the steps to the Turners' porch.

"Anytime you want to dig a movie, you just tell me," Bobby called.

One night he took me into the heart of the Horner Project.

The sky was a pink blanket behind the rooftops on Washington Boulevard. The children on the playground were hurrying through a last inning of softball, a last round of dodgeball. We walked into the hall on the first floor. There was a red-lighted EXIT sign above the door. The corridors were smudged and smelled of beer, but there was none of the filth and decay that you smelled in the tenement building on Jackson Boulevard. We climbed concrete steps, like the back staircase for employees in a hospital. Bobby ran up two at a time. We went up five stories and followed a maze of corridors. Bobby tapped on a door and we walked in.

The living room walls were concrete blocks painted canary yellow. A woman and some small children were watching television. The furniture was decent. These people could have afforded a house if they'd been able to find one.

"They in Boysie's room," the woman said over her shoulder.

Bobby led me down another concrete passage and we stepped into Boysie's tiny bedroom.

It was like stepping into a storm. The room was a blizzard of music. Lou Rawls was singing and the bass and percussion behind him seemed to be trying to break down the walls. The music was from a tape recorder.

Tommy and Al, the identical twins, and John and Boysie were sprawled on beds and chairs listening to the music. Their eyes rolled to Bobby, and four fists twitched in salute. John moved over and I sat down on the edge of one of the twin beds. I didn't know how to sit or what to do with my eyes. I watched the revolving reel of the tape recorder. Bobby leaned against a chest of drawers.

They were singing softly with Lou Rawls. They tapped their feet, and now and then their arms flared as though to illustrate a certain word or note.

The tape ran out and Boysie bounced off the bed and threaded the Temptations into the machine. "Now you gonna hear somethin," Bobby told me. Boysie hit a lever, and the Temptations sang. Heels tapped harder and fingers snapped. Boysie began to squirm on the bed. Suddenly he stood up next to Bobby. They began to sway in unison to the music. Tommy jumped up. The three filled the tiny floor. The Temptations moved on into "My Girl."

Bobby and Boysie and Tommy smiled at each other as though they shared a secret. Their eyes were half closed. The Temptations sang and the three swayed like supple stalks stirred by currents, rubbing softly against the music as it slid past.

I wanted to leap to the floor. But I didn't belong out there. I was lucky to be in the room.

Afterwards, as we walked back along Washington Boulevard, Bobby asked me who my favorite singer was. I thought about Judy Collins and Bob Dylan — I tried to remember when they had moved me as much as the Temptations had that night.

"I got a lot of favorites," I said.

The streetlights were on, and the pale yellow shone on the leaves. Bobby waved and jogged up the steps to his apartment building. He jogged gracefully, as though he were still dancing.

The Mile Square Federation was almost as ineffective as Virgil said it was. The officers, whose names were listed on the letterhead, never came to the office. Bobby and Virgil said they were all Uncle Toms. The place would have had to close without Bobby. Louis came in a few hours a week, and there was a girl who helped answer phones.

Stanley had launched his job program. He compiled a file of every business in the community and talked to the personnel managers. Most of them agreed to hire the people he sent to them. People started to come in about jobs. Stanley asked them to sit on a chair in front of his desk, interviewed them, and put their names in a file. They were all ages. Stanley must have filled a cabinet with his files. Every time someone called about a job, we referred him to Stanley, and Stanley grabbed the receiver and said, "Mile Square, Hastings speaking."

Bobby thought this was very funny. But Stanley was finding jobs. "You're an all right dude," Bobby told him.

Brett was the self-appointed Stokely Carmichael of our Vista team. "Do you know what it does to you, to see your own brother get his jaw broke right in front of you?" he would purr. He narrowed his eyes at Stanley and me as though we were the ones who had done it to his brother. Every time something displeased him he said, "It's the system. It's the whole jive system." I asked him what he meant by "the system," and he said "the whole white racist bag," or "the whole jive establishment." I wondered why Brett had joined Vista, which was rooted deep in the system. He claimed to have been in CORE and SNCC, and I couldn't see any militant leaving either of these and enlisting in a tame outfit like Vista. He didn't tell us what he was doing for his people all the hours he was gone. I thought he was out crisscrossing the ghetto on mysterious missions. Vista thought otherwise. They fired him in less than three weeks.

A few days after we got to the Turners' house, Wesley started to talk about the system too. He had grown up in a suburb of Pittsburgh, and I think he was surprised when his brothers on the West Side of Chicago didn't swarm out of the alleys to share their beer with him. Then he thought he saw why they didn't. One hot night we were sitting on the gritty wooden porch and Wesley murmured, "I admire you and Stanley for coming out here, but I don't think you belong here. As long as there are white Vistas at the Federation, the young militants are going to stay away." He started sleeping till eleven in the morning. The supervisors downtown found out. They let him sleep for a week, then fired him.

Brett and Wesley, like every black person in this country, had a right to be bitter. But Brett and Wesley wouldn't even help us answer housing complaints. They talked about revolution, they didn't make it. I bet they are still doing nothing, and still talking.

I stayed as close to Bobby as I could. I was supposed to be learning for the year ahead, and with him I could explore the ghetto and meet its people. We answered housing complaints. We roamed up and down Madison and Lake Streets and spoke to storekeepers about Stanley's job applicants. We sat in the office and talked to the people who came in out of the sun on Madison Street.

Bobby knew most of them. Some came for help, some came to pass time. It was shady and cool in the office. Madison Street looked white-hot through the open door and plate glass windows. A transistor radio crackled. "Light My Fire" was the number one song, and Jose Feliciano's sensual, nasal voice writhed in the shadows.

We really didn't know how to correct the outrages that had been done to the people who saw our signs in the window and came in. There was a file box on

Bobby's desk that held the names of people and organizations who could give us advice and sometimes help. At least once a day someone would come in and sit down in front of the desk. No matter how old, he would look tired and whipped, and he would look the same when he went out again into the awful heat. Maybe it helped to talk. I was never sure.

There were times when we could give stopgap help. One afternoon a man and woman came in. The man was wearing a white shirt with big red flowers stamped on it. The shirt was very dirty. They sat down and slumped forward.

"What's the matter?" Bobby said.

The woman stared at the floor while the man spoke. "We been sleepin in boxcars. We been sleepin in trailers. We ain't got nowhere to go. We ain't got nothin to eat."

We called the Salvation Army and asked them to give these people a bed for the night. There was no room. We called the Pacific Garden Mission on State Street, and a gentle voice on the other end told me to send them over. There would be a bed and a meal. We gave the man and woman bus fare and told them how to get there.

Anyone in America who really wants to can get a job and earn a living and buy a house, say the experts in the suburbs and small towns. The old couple scuffed out into the fading light as though a barrage of bombs had just gone off all around them.

One time a young unmarried mother came in. The

day before she had cashed her Aid to Dependent Children check. A man had pulled her into an alley and held a knife under her chin. She had given him the money. She wouldn't get another check for a month. She had two children. We called the Welfare office on Madison Street and persuaded them to give her emergency aid.

Late one afternoon a woman came in. If Bobby had been there, he might have known what to do. It was nearly five, and sun was slanting a luminous gold into Madison Street. I was sitting on top of the desk next to the door. Wesley was sitting in the desk chair. The woman lurched in and grabbed my wrists.

She couldn't have been forty, but she looked wilted and very old. She was wearing a bright blue dress covered with silver sequins. I will never forget that dress. It looked as though it had lain in a gutter through an all-night rain. She was a small woman with nice legs, and I could almost picture her as a cute housewife or an office girl. But last night, or last week, or perhaps for years, she had been wasted. She had been pumped and reamed and tasted all over and now, for a while at least, they had tossed her away.

"I'm so drunk," she said. Her voice was husky. The smell of whiskey rushed against my face.

I stood up and pushed her gently into a chair.

"I just need thirty-five cents," she rasped. "To get home. I got to get home. I got to take a bath."

"You need thirty-five cents?" I said. I was thinking I should try to keep her there till she was calmer.

"Honey, I so drunk. I want to take a bath, you know what I mean? I so drunk." Wesley sat behind the desk and stared straight ahead, and I wished if he were so goddamn intent on helping his people that he would at least give me an idea or two.

The woman pitched back up out of the chair and clawed at my shoulder. The whiskey smell came back like a hot wind. I eased her into the chair again, but she stumbled back up.

"I just got to get cleaned up."

Her voice trailed off and she looked down and studied her dress, as though she were seeing it for the first time. She held the skirt and shook it gently. She examined the dress. Her hands moved down, and suddenly she flipped the skirt up, as high as her breasts. She was wearing nothing under it. The tiny furry triangle between her legs looked so assailable and punishable that it was as though she had bared her insides to the edges of a broken bottle.

The dress came down, like a curtain.

"All right," I said. "I'll be glad to lend you thirty-five cents." I reached into my pocket. I had no change. I wasn't thinking very clearly. There was a dry cleaner next door, a white man. "Wait," I said to the woman. I went next door and got the man to change a dollar. When I got back, the woman was gone.

Sam Jefferson, like Bobby, had stopped breaking the law and was trying to help his people. Like Bobby, he was making a quixotic crusade on the West Side of Chicago. It seemed naïve, even to me. But no one laughed at them. Bobby and Sam could mix it up in an alley with anyone who wanted to jump.

"Crazy Sam, they used to call him," Bobby said. "First time I ever seen him he was bustin a car window with his hand. Just stuck his hand right through the glass." Sam had a long juvenile police record. He had helped some boys kick in the face of a white sailor on Madison Street, and during the first riot he had tried to organize a sniping attack. "What's happenin, Stokely?" people said to him on the street. But he had changed.

"There are good white cats and bad ones," he told me. "It's like this: you need us, and we need you."

Sam was working for the Chicago Federation of Settlements when I met him. It was a searing morning in early August. Bobby and I were lolling in the shadows at the back of the office. Sam stepped in out of the white light and peered around the room as though he were thinking of buying the place. He was wearing an untucked khaki shirt and sandals and he looked like a biblical character. Sam was skinny and bent and had a tuft of hair on his chin. He blinked and spotted Bobby.

"Brother Brassfield, what you doin, baby?" He shuffled over and sat down. Bobby introduced us.

"What is this place?" Sam asked, still measuring the office.

"Community work," Bobby said.

Sam told us about the Chicago Federation of

Settlements. He was supposed to go up to Michigan on a camping trip with some kids. He watched Stanley making phone calls at the front of the office.

"I think I'll try to give you all some help," Sam said. His voice was hoarse. "You all had any meetins lately?"

"Naw," Bobby said. "The officers get together once a month, but that ain't nothin. They ain't nothin but a bunch of damn Uncle Toms."

"Why don't we plan a meetin?" Sam said. "Get some of the young brothers in here and rap to them."

Next morning Sam and I walked up and down Madison Street handing out mimeographed sheets that announced a meeting at the office one week from that night. I had hesitated to go. I wasn't sure Sam wanted a white man with him. "You go on," Bobby had grinned. "I want to get you out of my hair for a while."

So Sam and I tucked the papers under our arms and set out. Sam would thrust a sheet at someone and say, "We gonna get it together, brother. Eight o'clock. I know I'll see you there." Two strong young men in orange and green jerseys accepted the leaflets and studied Sam as though he were asking them to buy vacuum cleaners. "Come and express your problems," Sam said. They stared politely, and walked on. Sam held up a paper to a kid sitting on top of a mailbox. The kid had a bushy natural. "Where is this place?" he asked. We were sixty feet from the office door.

Sam must have handed out five hundred leaflets that week. On the day of the meeting he told Bobby to introduce him and then let him run it. He said the first thing was to get people to state their problems. Once they got started, they would sense their strength as a group.

No one came at eight. Bobby, Sam, Stanley, Brett, Wesley and I waited as the sun sank and the lights flickered on. At eight fifteen Mr. and Mrs. Matthews, the old couple who had taken Bobby and me to their home for my first housing complaint, came in with their ragged little daughter. They sat down in the empty gallery of folding chairs as though they were waiting for an outbound train. At eight thirty a trickle began, till about half the seats were taken. No one looked under forty. They were all old and worn-out, like Mr. and Mrs. Matthews.

Sam didn't look disappointed. He stood in front of them and talked for twenty minutes. He wanted everyone to organize. Together they could stop Whitey. The numb faces stared at him. There was no place to go to complain about their troubles, so they had come here to listen to Sam, who was twenty and had a juvenile record that included assault with a deadly weapon. They wanted to get rid of the cockroaches and lower the rents they paid for their tiny, filthy apartments. None of them, not even Sam, knew what a small chance they had.

They filed silently out of the office. Sam said goodbye to us and walked out into the darkness.

Nobody got organized, but Sam didn't give up. He drifted away from the Chicago Federation of Settlements. He liked to work his own way. He was out in the streets at all times of day. He drank beer and smoked marijuana and sometimes got into hard drugs, and didn't eat as much as he needed. He coughed and his voice got weaker. He was nervous. His hands twitched and his legs jiggled. I bought him meals when I could. We would eat at a place across the street from the office. You could get a plate heaped with soul food — meat, corn, greens, cornbread, a piece of pie — for a little more than a dollar. The room was greasy and hot, and the food was delicious.

Sam decided the best thing he could do was talk to his people. He hung around the streets after dark. He tried to talk people out of fighting and stealing. It sounds funny, but if you had seen Sam you wouldn't have even felt like smiling. He was dignified and alert, and he had soul. I doubt that anyone on the West Side ever followed his advice, but I know that no one laughed at him.

He carried a notebook and asked people to write down some of their ideas. He would spend a whole night gathering this material, then bring it to the office in the morning. He brought pages of lines scrawled by bartenders and high school poets. We typed them on stencils, ran them on the mimeograph machine, and stapled the pages together. Sam named our publication the *Black Liberator*. He chose the articles we printed and wrote one or two himself. Then we would hand out the *Black Liberator* to passers-by on Madison Street.

Sam had been arrested inside a grocery store the third night of the April riot. They had charged him with burglary and inciting to riot. He was to appear in court the last week of August.

Sam went over with me many times what happened that night in the store. It was a white-owned supermarket. It had been broken into and looted, and its floor was strewn with slashed cartons and broken bottles. Everything valuable had been taken. Sam was walking the streets, and he noticed some kids in the store pawing through the litter. There were two sets of swinging glass doors, and Sam had pushed open the first and called to the kids from the foyer. He told them to get out before they got shot. While he was speaking a brace of policemen shoved him into the store and ordered him and the others to stand against the wall. They were searched and arrested.

Bobby said the charges were very serious. I telephoned the Community Legal Counsel downtown. The man I talked to told me that they only had time to take cases that could set new precedents and shatter old ones. There wasn't enough potential in Sam's case.

Bobby and I went with Sam to the grocery store. It was an air-conditioned supermarket, and it was in business again. We walked through the foyer where Sam had been grabbed, and he pointed to the concrete wall where they had been lined up and frisked. Where those boys had flattened out and reached toward the ceiling, there were baskets of rubber balls, a couple of bubble gum machines, and the edge of the bread shelves. We asked to speak to the manager.

He was a shy-looking white man wearing glasses and a black knitted tie. He was very polite. Bobby let me talk to him. It was the only time Bobby ever let me take over. The white grocer listened and shook his head from time to time. I told him we hoped he would drop charges.

"Well gee," he said. "I wish I could help you. But we aren't the ones who press charges. The City of Chicago is pressing charges against you."

"Oh."

"Gee," the manager said. "I'm sorry it happened this way." He glanced around the store. There were long lines at each checkout counter. "You know, we lost an awful lot of money. We're only just getting back on our feet."

"I know," I said, "but your store was picked clean before Sam ever got here."

"Gee, I realize this," he said. "But there just isn't anything I can do."

Bobby and I went with Sam to the criminal court at 2600 California Avenue. It was a massive stone building with airy halls and courtrooms on every floor. We took an elevator up three floors and found the room. The judge was hearing the case of a black kid about Sam's age. The judge sat way up behind his desk and

squinted down at the accused, who gazed at his feet.
The D.A. and the city lawyer stood on each side of him.
and the uniformed bailiff rocked on spread legs, his
hands behind his back. Bobby and Sam and I found
seats on one of the empty wooden benches.

"Samuel Jefferson!"

It was Sam's turn. Bobby and I followed him up to
the spot below the judge. They let us stand behind him
while the charges were read. He had to listen and make
his plea.

The lawyer who was supposed to help Sam was a trim
dark man with a bald head and an aggressive chin. He
wanted Sam to plead guilty.

"Jefferson," he said, "I can get you four months and
two years' probation if you plead guilty. But if you try
to fight this thing, you haven't got a chance."

"He didn't steal anything and he didn't incite anyone," I said.

The city lawyer looked at me as though I had just
asked for one of his best cigars. "What was he doing
in the store in the first place? The thing to do is stay out
of the store in the first place."

"So he asked for the charges because he was in the
store?"

The lawyer turned to Sam. "The penalty is two to fifteen years. That's in a state pen. You want that?"

"But I ain't done nothin," Sam said. "You want me to
say I done somethin I ain't done."

The lawyer shrugged. "You don't have a chance the

other way." He glanced at his watch. "You think about
it."

We walked out into the hall. The windows at the end
were open, and the factories sent white and black smoke
into the blue August sky.

"Motherfucker wants me to cop a plea," Sam said.

"What are you going to do?" I said.

"I don't know," Sam said. "I don't know what I'm
gonna do."

"Fight it," Bobby said.

"But man, he talkin about fifteen years," Sam said.

"He tryin to scare you," Bobby said. "You never get
more than five."

"Shit, you think I want five?"

"The four months wouldn't be anything," I said.

"Yeah, but two years' probation," Sam said. "Man,
you can't do nothin when you on probation. If they pick
you up for anythin, you gone."

I had learned how capriciously the police stop black
kids on the street.

"Anyhow, it's the idea of it," Sam said. His little voice
croaked and his skinny hands squeezed pieces of air. "I
don't want to say I done somethin I ain't done."

We went back in. When the judge summoned Sam
and asked him how he pleaded he said, "Not guilty."
The lawyer glanced at me as though I were a parent
letting my six-year-old skydive. He must have assumed I
knew better because I was white.

The judge continued the case until late in September.

Before I left Chicago I tried to find a lawyer for Sam. None of the legal aid outfits would take the case. Sam went back to work. He didn't know what he was going to do. Once he said he might leave the city. I never found out what happened to him. He had no address. I wrote a couple of times to Bobby, but either he had moved, or he was too busy to answer.

Fate had made cruel arrangements for Sam. How would you like to be told that the best thing you could do, whether you were innocent or guilty, was to say you were guilty? How would you like to be told to cop a plea?

"Let's go over to Old Town and see what the hippies are doin," Bobby said.

He was lying on the floor in front of the television in the Turners' little sitting room. We were watching the Democratic Convention. The Democrats were getting ready to nominate Hubert Humphrey. The night before there had been a battle between the police and a crowd that had assembled to protest the ideas of men like Hubert Humphrey. They had fought in Lincoln Park in Old Town, on the North Side of the city.

"Sure," I said.

Stanley wanted to come with us, and out on Washington Boulevard near the Horner Project we met Bobby's friend Thomas.

"What you doin?" Thomas asked.

"We goin over to Old Town to check out the hippies," Bobby grinned. So Thomas came along. He was a quiet kid. He wore a white jacket that made him look like a pharmacist.

Lincoln Park was a huge, rolling lawn speckled with trees. We got there at ten. It was the end of August, and the night was cool. The people had lighted campfires on the grass. Their forms were black against the bright orange of the fires, and they sat cross-legged, gazing into the flames like soldiers resting before a battle. Some strummed guitars. The sweet, earthy smell of marijuana hung in the damp air. Groups of older people wandered around looking at the kids, like tourists in the flea market in Madrid.

Bobby and Thomas and Stanley and I roamed up and down the grassy slopes and looked at the people. They were chanting around some of the fires; from somewhere came the hollow throb of a bongo drum. It was primitive and warlike. Bobby seemed aroused. He laughed and shouted and pranced in and out of crowds.

The city ordinance said that the park had to be empty after eleven. At ten thirty, people started to leave. First went the well-dressed older white people. At quarter to, some of the young people drifted toward the streets.

"I think we ought to leave," I said.

"I ain't goin nowhere," Bobby said. He jittered like a nervous racehorse.

"What do you think, Stanley?" I said. They had arrested hundreds the night before.

"We'll be all right," Stanley said.

"I don't know," I said. I was afraid they might surround us.

"You can go," Bobby said. "Man, go on if you want to." He was watching me carefully.

"What the hell," I said. "Sure, I'll stay."

It got closer and closer to eleven. The bongo drum thundered a crescendo. The people around the fires stood up. Everyone was peering into the darkness beyond the edges of the park. Someone climbed onto a makeshift platform above a fire and shouted to the crowd at his feet, the flames tossing wriggling shadows on his face. No one knew where the police were. Eleven o'clock. Fear hung like humidity.

Someone spotted the police. They were gathering on a hill at the east edge of the park just inside Lake Shore Drive. There was a rush to see them. They were spilling out of cruisers and paddywagons and gathering in a herd that swelled and swelled. They wore light blue shirts and powder blue helmets. The helmets were like hundreds of identical pastel bubbles under the arclights.

The kids started to set up trash barrels and pieces of scrap metal. I don't know where they found so much, but they built a barricade and ranged themselves behind it like *sans-culottes* in the streets of Paris. They shouted and pounded on the metal barrels, and the policemen gazed down at them from the hill. Bobby and Thomas and Stanley and I stayed in the rear ranks.

At midnight an announcement rolled down the slope out of a bullhorn. THIS IS A WARNING. ALL

PEOPLE MUST LEAVE THE PARK. ANYONE WHO DOES NOT LEAVE THE . . .

They smothered the loudspeaker with chants. "Hell no, we won't go! Hell no, we won't go!" The cops waited another five minutes and made one more try. THIS IS THE LAST WARNING . . . But they killed it with shouting and hammering on the barricade.

The army on the hill deployed in a long line. They were fitting gas masks on their faces. I had seen pictures of gas masks in World War I photographs. The kids howled and beat on the barricade. They were really going to stay. We four peered into the darkness. The retreat looked good.

And then they came down the hill. They came quietly. They trudged, a sky-blue phalanx with gas masks and clubs, and the kids stood their ground until the canisters of tear gas began to fall. We four danced back, beyond the blue-white clouds, and watched the gas hit the kids behind the barricade. Some ran. Others slumped and waited for the cops to split their heads and haul them to the paddywagons. The gas spread over the slopes. The cops were silhouetted, burly giants with sticks in their fists.

They were very close to us. People were running. We spun and sprinted up a slope to Clark Street. The gas pushed up the hill and billowed into the street. We crossed, dodging cars, and ran around a corner. My eyes burned and my nose and throat felt as though fire had been poured into them. We ran until we had es-

caped the gas. The side street was quiet. It was lined
with trees. There were three black kids there. They had
also outrun the gas, and they choked and coughed and
held handkerchiefs to their noses.

"God*damn*," Bobby wheezed.

Stanley laughed.

We peered up the avenue toward the brightly lit intersection of Wells and Clark Streets. The crowd was re-
forming. We breathed the gas out of our noses and
throats.

"Come on," Bobby said.

The protesters controlled the intersection. It was
blocked by cars parked at angles. The traffic was strung
out under the lights along Clark and Wells Streets. The
kids were making another stand. I saw one with stream-
ing yellow hair and a bandage wrapped around his
skull, soaked with blood. "There's blood on the streets,"
he was shouting. "Blood on the streets!"

Suddenly the police charged again. They came from
the north. There was a flurry and a sudden, general
rush. Then you heard the cops swearing and the clubs
cracking on heads. They ran everyone out of the intersection. I saw a cop catch a kid my age and knock him
down with one swing. The kid rose to his knees and the
cop hit him twice on the head and he stretched out like a
cat going to sleep.

Bobby and Thomas and Stanley and I jogged south
with the mob.

Wells Street in Old Town looks like a strip out of the

1890s. Ornate bars, lighted arcades, and Parisian coffeehouses do business with students and middle-aged swingers. The police swept down Wells Street in a wave, pushing a couple of hundred of us before them. People stepped out onto the street from the bars to watch us go by. It would have been easy to get caught if the police came the moment you stepped outside. At the streets that cut into Wells, policemen were planted with their clubs. They didn't let anyone slip away.

I should have seen what they were doing. But with the thrill of outrunning the police, the gay, embattled mood of the protesters, the red and orange lights in the bars, and the crisp night air, I wasn't thinking. We walked for about half an hour. Then suddenly the singing and the shouting stopped.

Ahead, strung out across the street, the helmeted men with their black clubs faced us. Behind, the sweepers were moving up fast. There was going to be a big bust on Wells Street. They were going to get almost two hundred of us.

I glimpsed Stanley. We were on the sidewalk near a mesh fence. I was having trouble breathing. Stanley's cartoon eyebrows arched, and even then he seemed to be smiling. "Don't worry," he said. "We can get out of this." *Excuse me, officer, but we're Vista volunteers and we're here by accident.*

The chasers were there. The trap closed. There was a panicked flurry. We had no place to go. The cops swore. The clubbing sounded like axes in the woods.

I saw Bobby and Thomas disappear through an opening in the fence. There was a parking lot behind it. At the back was another wire fence. It was more than ten feet high. Bobby scrambled up like a monkey. Thomas followed. I paused in front of the fence. The hammering and grunting and swearing were all around me. I grabbed the fence and sailed up. Others were trying. The cops were snatching them off the fence. At the top there were three strands of barbed wire. I tried to throw myself clear of it, but it caught my stomach and wrist as I went over.

I landed on all fours on more asphalt. Several dark shapes were slithering into the shadows on La Salle Street. Bobby and Thomas were there. They were dusting their pants. La Salle Street was empty and still. Everyone but us had slipped away.

"Where's Stanley?" Bobby said. I had been the last one over the fence.

"I don't think he made it," I said. My flannel shirt was ripped and there was a bloody gap in my wrist.

We walked cautiously around the corner to Wells Street. The police had everyone in a herd and were loading them into paddywagons. We spotted Stanley. He stood with his hands in his pockets. His eyebrows looked stunned, not happy.

The cops had the area cordoned. "Move along before we take you in too," they growled. We walked on.

We got home at three in the morning. The Horner Project was a great blue shadow with two or three lights, like an ocean liner in the night. Thomas nodded to us, lifted his fist in salute, and disappeared. Bobby and I crossed Washington Boulevard and split up.

I slid out of my clothes and crawled into bed. I felt as though I had just played a thirty-inning ball game. I tried to remember climbing the fence. It was as though I had been unconscious. The only thing I could remember was landing on all fours on the asphalt on the other side, and scrambling away while the clubs cracked against heads on the other side of the wire. I had felt like a cat as I landed.

My wrist and stomach were scarred for nearly half a year. Bobby and Thomas had clambered over the vicious little barbs without a scratch. It must have taken a lot of practice to be able to do that.

Stanley was kept in jail for the night and charged with disorderly conduct. His father in New Jersey was furious and hired a lawyer, who charged $250 and lost the case. The judge fined Stanley five dollars and sent him home.

We stepped out onto the porch of the Turners' house lugging our suitcases. A chilly wind blew through the leaves of the elms on Washington Boulevard. The sky was the color of skim milk. Bobby and Stanley and I sat on the wooden railing and waited for our ride to the airport.

"This is kind of sad," Bobby said.

"I wish you could come," I said.

Stanley stared down the boulevard.

"Listen, man," Bobby said. He squinted seriously through the thick lenses of his glasses. "My people can be pretty mean sometimes. If things get bad up there in Detroit, don't you all try to be no heroes or nothin. Don't be afraid to pull up if you have to, you hear?"

"Sure."

A taxi veered out of the flow of traffic and stopped at the curb. We gathered up the suitcases and hobbled down the steps and heaved them into the trunk of the cab.

I took Bobby's hand. It was hard and warm and dry.

"Take care of yourself, old man," he said softly. He shook hands with Stanley. "Good luck, baby."

"Good luck."

We slid into the back seat and slammed the door. Bobby stood on the curb with his hands rammed into the tight blue-jean pockets. The driver glanced over his shoulder and headed out into the traffic. I turned and watched Bobby. He stood still, staring after the cab. I watched him until he was hidden by the porches.

II

That's What They'll Call You

TWO

THE CITIZENS of Detroit were happy. Their Tigers were about to win the American League pennant. They hadn't won it for more than twenty years. Even the people who knew nothing about baseball were waiting for the Tigers to wrap it up. Stickers on back fenders said SOCK IT TO 'EM, TIGERS! Photographs of Denny McLain and Willie Horton were taped to store windows. Cardboard tigers and stuffed tigers and plaster tigers brandished bats and bared fangs on every counter and display case.

It was like the fever in Chicago during the convention. But Chicago had been blown apart by fraud and hatred and politics. Detroit was joined in the boisterous adoration of its baseball team.

There were five Vista volunteers at the YMCA. We were waiting to be sent into the ghetto. Our sponsoring agency was the Detroit Commission on Children and Youth. The Commission office was on the twenty-fifth floor of the Broderick Tower, up among the gray tops of the skyscrapers of downtown Detroit. There were two branch offices: one on the East Side, one on the West

Side. These outposts were dingy little rented offices out where the poverty and violence were. I was going to the West Side with one other Vista, a girl. The other four boys at the Y were on their way to the East Side.

"You realize," said Willie Mack Thomas, "that there's a lot of hostility toward white Vistas, don't you?"

We were sitting around a table in the conference room of the office in the Broderick Tower. The city sprawled below us in a hazy gray tangle of fumes and rooftops.

"There's been plenty of opposition," Willie went on. His voice was firm and even, yet soft. He had a handsome red-black face with a sickle-shaped mustache and natural hair. He and Mrs. Gloria Wattles and Chuck Lewis, the head of the Commission, sat at the head of the table. Gloria ran the East Side office, Willie the West. I would be working under Willie.

A hand went up. "Uh, how bad is this hostility?"

"You never know," Gloria said. "You're not a brother and you never will be. But if you show you're for real, you'll be all right."

"It's something you got to get used to," Willie said. He was used to a lot of things. Chuck Lewis sat back with his chin in his hand and watched.

"Any more questions?"

We stared at the table. "All right," Chuck said. "You're on your way."

Willie Thomas got out of the car. The landlord was waiting at the steps to the apartment building. It was brick, two stories high, with peeling, mustard-colored window casings. The September afternoon was hot and bright.

"Are you Mr. Hunter?" Willie said.

"Yeah." Mr. Hunter was staring at me. A charred stump in overalls. His head was square and grizzled, and he had a mustache and smoked a cigar. He stared at me as though Willie had brought along a pet kangaroo.

"I'm Mr. Thomas of the Commission on Children and Youth." Willie stuck out his hand and Mr. Hunter took it suspiciously. They stood there on the cement walk in the sunlight and Willie explained who I was and what I was doing. Mr. Hunter put the cigar in his mouth and started up the steps. He pushed open the door and led us down a cool, dark hall to a door at the back of the building. He unlocked the door and we stepped into the apartment.

The walls were mustard colored and the floor was brown linoleum. There was one room with a double bed, a frayed green sofa, a bedside table, and two chests of drawers. The kitchen was narrow and tiny, with a rickety gas stove. The bathroom was the size of a closet. The apartment smelled like gas and Lestoil.

"Sixty-five a month, you said?" Willie ran his gaze up and down the walls.

"That's right. Utilities included." Mr. Hunter sat

down on the sofa and took the cigar out of his mouth. He studied me. "I'm right surprised to see a white boy," he said. " 'Course I don't care none what color a man's skin is. So long as I get my rent, I don't care."

"I'm sure we can rely on the checks," Willie said. He was wearing a jacket and tie and looked very respectable.

"You ain't gonna carry on and make a lot of noise?" Mr. Hunter rammed the cigar back in and squinted at me.

"No sir," I said.

"Well," he said biting the cigar. "You look like a nice boy. I guess you can have it." I gave him sixty-five dollars and he handed me the key.

Willie drove me to Sears to buy sheets and a pillow, and to Goodwill Industries to buy pots and pans and plates. Goodwill sells secondhand, and trains and pays mentally retarded people to stock the shelves and punch the cash register. Everything they sell is donated. The warehouse was full of poor black people pawing through the boxes and mounds of pots, can openers, electric radios, and jelly glasses. I felt as poor as any of them. I had about forty dollars, and I didn't know when my next check was coming. I was going to be making fifty dollars a week. I bought two saucepans, a frying pan with a broken handle, three plates, three cups, three glasses, three forks, three knives, three spoons, and a spatula. It all cost three dollars and twenty-four cents.

There were long shadows and a flaming western sky when Willie left me in front of the apartment building.

"Are you going to be all right?" he said.

"Sure."

"I'll see you tomorrow."

"All right."

He put the car in gear and left me. I climbed the steps and put my shoulder against the door and shoved it open. My arms were full of the things I had bought. A light was on in the hall, a bare bulb spreading pale yellow on the blue-green walls. I unlocked my door and dropped everything on the bed. The pans clattered. I had to get some food.

I went out again. The apartment building stood on Webb Avenue, near Hamilton Street, on a block of brick apartment buildings. I turned north on Hamilton and headed for the Wrigley supermarket. Hamilton was like Madison Street. It was wide and busy, lined with shops and barrooms. People spilled out of doorways and stood talking on the sidewalk in the hot early evening. You could see where the riot had been last summer, by the scorched buildings with plywood patches over doors and windows.

Wrigley was about a half a mile away. Before I got there a couple of kids about my age wearing African shirts stopped me.

"Hey, honkie, you got a match?"

"Sorry," I said.

"That's too bad, man. Now if you had a reefer for me, I'd say you was a blue-eyed soul brother."

I shook my head and walked on. They must have thought I was selling marijuana. They must have thought I had a good reason for being alone on Hamilton Street.

Wrigley was a big, dirty supermarket that charged more than any supermarket outside the inner city. I was the only white person in the place. I grabbed a cart and filled it with basics — butter, salt, napkins — and added enough for a couple of meals. It cost more than ten dollars and I was down to less than thirty dollars. I pressed the bags against my chest and trudged back to the apartment. It was getting dark and the streetlights were blinking on.

The apartment was bare and silent. I opened a window and let in the sounds of traffic and shouts from Hamilton Street. I set a can of spaghetti on the table. Then I discovered I didn't have any matches. I swore softly. I didn't want to go outside again.

But there were no matches in any of the drawers, so I went out and crossed Webb. There was a gas station on the corner, a big one with huge fluorescent lights and an office with glass walls. A kid in blue jeans was sitting on an empty coke case. He measured me. I asked him if he had a match.

"No, man. I ain't got a single match." I thought I spotted the glimmer of a smile.

His boss, a burly man in a T-shirt, came out of the office.

"I just moved in across the street," I said. "I don't have any matches."

The man shook his head. "Thanks anyway," I said. They must have had some matches in that gas station. I walked a short block north and went into a little grocery store. The swarthy, dirty-looking white man behind the counter sold me a box of matches.

I got back and closed the door, letting the lock catch with a snap. I picked up the can of spaghetti. I had no can opener.

Jesus, no. I wasn't going out again. I found some scissors and attacked the can of spaghetti. I jammed the point through the top of the can and tore. The smell of tomato leaked out. I ripped and gouged until I had a ragged slot big enough for the spaghetti to ooze through.

After dinner I lay down on the double bed. I had a little transistor radio. The Tigers were playing Washington. McLain had won his thirtieth game, and the team was romping to the pennant. I lay on my back staring at the ceiling. The radio sputtered in the silence of the apartment. I would have to have my record player sent.

There were shouts and car horns on Hamilton. Kids walked under the window in the alley. Gravel and broken glass crunched under their feet. I could hear every word they said. The Tigers were winning when I fell asleep.

The West Side office of the Commission on Children and Youth was a complex of little rooms above a grocery store on the corner of Fullerton and Livernois. It was stuffed with gray metal desks, typewriters, telephones and filing cabinets. In the front room a bulletin board was covered with clippings about black people. There was a photograph poster of Martin Luther King. Everyone who worked in the office was black.

Willie Thomas had his own small office. Erlinda Ngayan was already there, sitting in a chair pulled up facing Willie's desk. Erlinda was the other Vista. She was a genteel, unresponsive little Philippine girl with very tan skin and very black hair.

Willie didn't know what to do with us. He hadn't ordered any Vista volunteers. We had been requisitioned by Chuck Lewis, the head of the Commission. Chuck always worked downtown. We had been sent to Willie, and he leaned back in his chair and thought about what he might do with us. The morning sun emphasized the red in his dark skin. There was a photograph of Rap Brown on the wall behind him.

"What do you think you might like to do?" He wanted to get back to work.

"I wonder if we could get into a school," I said.

The junior high school sat stubbornly on Twelfth Street. It had survived the riot, which had raged all around it. It was surviving the insults of the ghetto. Rocks were thrown at it, .22 bullets were fired through its windows, obscenities were scrawled on its walls, and now and then some kid had tried to set fire to it. But it sat there, and another school year was beginning when Erlinda and I walked into the office with Willie Thomas.

It was like any school office. The wooden floor was scuffed and the secretaries looked bored. There were four chairs along one wall, two of them occupied by kids. They sat hunched forward with their heads in their hands and stared sullenly at the floor.

A secretary led us to the principal's office, a small room adjacent to the main office.

"I'm Stephen Davidson." He stood up and shook hands all around. He wore glasses that looked thick enough to be bullet proof. "Sit down." He had a diffident smile, as though we had discovered him doing something wrong. "We're glad to have you. We will offer you any assistance we can."

"Very good," Willie said. He smiled like the man on TV who has just found a cure for his sore throat.

"When can we start?" I said.

"I'll see the guidance counselor today," Mr. Davidson said. "I'll have him make a list of students and set up schedules for you." He smiled meekly. "Do you, ah, really want the worst we've got?"

"Sure," I said quickly. What was the point, otherwise?

"We'll refer boys to you," he said, "and girls to you, Miss Ngayan."

"Fine," I said.

We stood up and everyone shook hands again. "You should be able to begin tomorrow," Mr. Davidson said.

Out in the hall the kids were changing classes. They spilled out of the rooms and poured down the halls. Their faces were a spectrum of browns, from blue-black to tawny café-au-lait. The boys were dressed two ways. They wore high-cut sneakers, overalls, and sweatshirts with sleeves torn off at the shoulders. Or they were smartened up in green, blue, and yellow slacks, cashmere sweaters, and black shoes, pointed and polished. The girls, wrapped in tight skirts, minced along in white sneakers. There were a lot of sweethearts. The boys talked and gestured while the girls watched out of the corners of their eyes, smiling as though they didn't believe it but liked it anyway. The school also held elementary schoolers. Their rooms were all in one end of the building, but they rubbed against the junior high. It was strange to see the tall, sullen kids of fifteen walking among their little first and second grade brothers.

I said I'd walk home. I wanted to see the neighborhood. Willie and Erlinda got in the car. Erlinda was living in the home of some friends of Willie's. They were a middle-aged couple with no children. They lived on Edison near Twelfth Street. It was a block of handsome brick houses surrounded by lawns and elm trees, a dab of black prosperity less than a mile from the street corner where the riot began.

They left me on the curb on Twelfth Street. It was a brilliant September morning, close to eighty-five de-

grees. I examined the outside of the school. It was cubic
and flat-roofed, with a yellow and gray façade and huge
modern windows. Next to it was an empty lot of dirt and
cinders, where the teachers parked their cars. Beyond
the lot were the houses on the next block. They were
two-story wood frame, tidy but decrepit.

I crossed Twelfth Street. A few blocks south began
the dirty barrooms and hotels and stores, the brick tenement buildings and the pool halls. The whores paraded
there, and the hustlers pushed every game that the city
had taught them. Whiskey bottles littered the sidewalks.
I drove down Twelfth Street many times that year, and
it always made me think. Nothing I had ever done had
required the wits and the courage it took to live in the
Twelfth Street ghetto. And there were thousands of
black people doing it. I admired every one of them.

I took the side street that joined Twelfth and Woodrow Wilson. There were some trees here. The porches
sagged; a screen door leaned like a cripple against the
wall. People lounged on the shady porches and studied
me as I walked by.

I turned south on Woodrow Wilson, where I had
more than half a mile to walk. I would get to know that
strip very well.

It was a wide, shadeless avenue. It had a couple of
grocery stores, a laundromat, a dry cleaner, a hardware
store, and several barrooms. The stores were dark and
low-ceilinged. The bars were windowless, with concrete
walls. They looked like bomb shelters. Every morning at

eight thirty as I walked to school I would see old men slipping in and out of the bars. The doors swung open and poured the smell of beer and the beat of soul music onto the sidewalk. The interiors were dark as caves.

The stores had flats above them. Doorways opened onto the sidewalk and narrow stairs led up to filthy, rat-infested homes. From the sidewalk along Woodrow Wilson, the windows looked gaping and mournful.

There were brick apartment buildings too. They were massive blocks with tin vacancy signs hanging next to the doors. The bricks were blackened, like the bricks of a hearth.

I inspected everything. There were few people on the street. A lot of them were old. There were not enough night spots to attract the gangs and the hungry cats with keen eyes. They would be a block over, on Twelfth Street. Still, I would have to be careful.

At Woodrow Wilson and Webb I passed the Metropolitan and Crittenton hospitals. Crittenton was a maternity hospital. They were modern complexes surrounded by asphalt parking lots, and it was comforting to see them beside all the baking squalor.

I turned east on Webb Avenue and crossed the John C. Lodge Expressway on an overpass. The Lodge Expressway was one of the chief arteries of the city. Thousands of cars from suburbia drove past to and from work each day, whisking just below Woodrow Wilson and Twelfth Street. Then I was on my stretch of Webb, with the brick apartment buildings and the cars parked tightly along the curb.

It was exactly a mile from the school to my home. All year I would be walking that mile. I would be walking it without Bobby Brassfield.

I unlocked the apartment. A cockroach scurried across the bathroom floor. I could hear the refrigerator buzzing and the clock ticking, and I opened the window to let in some air and noise.

THREE

THE SCHOOL LIBRARY was a long, sun-filled room over-loaded with books. It looked down from the second floor to the cindery playground. In the fall, the gym classes played touch football out there. From the library windows, it was difficult to spot any organization in the games. The teams squared off in confused, ragged formations. Someone centered the ball. There was a flurry of arms and legs, some shrill curses, and someone would launch the ball. Usually no one caught it. There were plenty of hips and elbows, and fights would flare. Then the white gym teacher would trot over and pull the fighters apart.

The library was used more than most are, in inner-city schools. The librarian was a cheerful young white man who knew a lot about children's literature and was good at helping kids find the right books. He hung pictures and displays — animals, clowns, knights — most of them for the elementary schoolers. He worked hard on these surroundings.

Erlinda and I waited for our students in the library.

We didn't have much idea of what our program would be, but we wanted to begin tutoring and see what would develop.

The first kid I talked to was Taylor Smith. Taylor sauntered into the library that first morning, studied the room from the doorway, and sloped over to me.

"You Mr. Hough?"

"That's right."

"Mr. Gordon sent me up to see you." Mr. Gordon was the guidance counselor.

"Sit down," I said. We sat across from each other at one of the yellow varnished tables. Taylor was a tall, husky boy of fifteen. He had a huge, sudden smile that transformed his whole face. He was wearing a blue cashmere sweater and yellow pants.

"We're going to work as fast as you want to," I said. "We're going to do stuff you like. When you find a book or a magazine or something you'd like to read, bring it in and we can work on it."

Taylor yawned and stared out the window. The sky was a hard blue. In the distance above the tarpaper roofs rose the Sears Building. It had a panel that flashed the time, then the temperature in yellow numbers.

"You got any questions?" I said.

Taylor shook his head.

I had a couple of eighth-grade math books. "You know anything about positive and negative numbers?"

Taylor shook his head and tilted back his chair and

watched me. He smiled faintly, as though I were reading the lines of Polonius or Falstaff. It wasn't what usually made him laugh, but it was amusing.

"Positive numbers," I began, "are numbers with a value greater than zero. Like two, that's two more than zero, right?" The librarian was stacking books across the room. Erlinda was talking softly with a girl at another table. "Negative numbers are less than zero. Negative two, that's two less than zero." I peered into Taylor's face. "You see that?"

"Nope."

I met a lot of them that first week. They were sent by the guidance counselor, or they heard about me and wandered in to see what was happening. They sat and talked, or let me tutor them in math and English. Their teachers didn't want them. They were the punks and misfits, the two or three bad ones in every class. They were supposed to be with me one period a day, but they stayed longer than that. I talked to their teachers, and they said I could have any of those kids as long as I wanted. The principal said I could give them their marks.

All the kids I tutored had ignored school work for three, four, maybe ten years. They were big boys, nearly physically mature. At fifteen, they had smoked marijuana, made love, been arrested, fought, and known people who had been murdered. They had active, alert minds. But they read like fourth graders.

I concentrated on reading at first. I tried some poems — Robert Frost, black poets like Langston Hughes — and I tried a book of adaptations of the Greek myths. They liked these. We were usually groups of three or four. They would take turns reading paragraphs aloud, and I would correct them and fill in the words they didn't know. I didn't teach phonics. I had never been instructed on how to teach reading, never taken a course in education. But slowly they learned to read.

They weren't embarrassed about their reading. If they had considered it a weakness, they would have tackled it. They were smart enough to. They remembered any word they were told. I wouldn't have dared tell them they couldn't fight, or couldn't make it with the girls, but I didn't mind handing out advice concerning reading.

They didn't seem to care what we read. Reading was reading. We plowed into the American history book, because I gave marks in history. I explored the poetry shelf and found plenty of good poems with easy words. I found books for sixth graders about King Arthur, John Henry, and Yankee whaling.

We would sit around a table, take turns reading, and chat. I tried to get them to talk about the books, or about themselves. They told me plenty. As soon as the word got around we were joined by outsiders, class-skippers or kids off the streets who didn't even go to school.

I didn't teach them much. But it was more than they would have had in regular classrooms. They were through with those.

The young white teacher was shoving Rick Smith out of the classroom, and Rick picked up an iron tripod that was leaning against the wall in the hall. The teacher froze. Behind him the kids surged through the doorway.

Rick held the tripod like a baseball bat and swung. The teacher leaped back and the iron clattered against the concrete wall. The class shrieked. Rick dropped the tripod and started after the teacher just as the history teacher darted around the corner and put a full nelson on him. The history teacher was black, a big man with a mustache. Rick squirmed and tried to yank his arms out of the lock, and they slid to the floor. The assistant principal came around the corner. It was his job to clean up these things. The two of them hauled Rick to his feet. The teacher who had been attacked stood with his arms hanging like rags. His lips were white.

"You got it comin," Rick hissed. "Baby, you got it comin." He was panting and glistening drops rolled down his rigid, dark face. The teacher stared at him.

"Let's go, Rick," the assistant principal said softly. He was a white man, thin and wiry and strong. The kids were afraid of him. He and the history teacher dragged Rick up the stairs toward the office.

The teacher turned to his students and waved at them like a shepherd herding sheep. "Back in the room, back in the room." They withdrew with insolent hesitation. He was beaten.

"Hey." He was calling me. "Will you watch my class for me?" His lips were the color of chalk and his hands trembled.

"All right," I said.

He went up the stairs toward the office and I went into his room. The kids were talking loudly. There was a lot of laughing. A big, burly kid ambled past me.

"What happened?" I asked him.

He paused and stared at me. "What you askin me for?"

"I was just wondering what happened," I said.

"You just be cool, or they gonna come back and get you next," he rumbled.

That was the year's first assault on a teacher. I didn't see all of them. But the story always flashed around the school, and I picked it up from my students. Once a black science teacher ordered a student out of the hall. The teacher had a yardstick, and he flicked it at the kid's thigh. There was a stack of cases of empty pop bottles next to a door, and the kid grabbed a coke bottle by the neck and shattered it against the wall. Leveling the jagged glass at the teacher's groin he began to circle, whispering, "Come on, motherfucker, come on and get what you got comin." One of the gym teachers sneaked up behind him and knocked the bottle away with a karate chop. The kid whirled and sprinted out before anyone could catch him. He called over his shoulder that he was coming back with a gun. It was his last day of school. The police couldn't find him, and we never saw him again. My kids were surprised. They said he wasn't the kind to do something like that.

A white teacher only a year older than I really got it. I heard the story from a boy named Leon. The teacher was blond and blue-eyed and very energetic. He was standing in front of his class and suddenly a few of the kids snickered. The teacher followed their eyes and discovered a lighted cigarette on the floor just inside the door. He stepped out into the hall and spotted Leon.

"Come here," he said.

Leon sloped over and the teacher grabbed him by the upper arm.

Leon glared at the hand on his arm. "Man, what you doin?"

The three who had tossed the cigarette clattered down the stairs. They had all been expelled several weeks ago. The teacher let go of Leon and grabbed one of them. The kid twisted and hit the teacher on the chest. They lurched against the wall, wrestling; another reached back and threw a terrific punch flush on the teacher's temple. The teacher shuddered and rolled away, and they hurled him to the floor and tried to stomp him. The assistant principal skidded up to save him, and the kids scattered. They had been recognized, though. The police picked them up and put them in a house of correction for several months.

The other one I saw was between women. I heard

that sound out in the hall, the shrill, electric wail of a fight crowd. I got up and went out. It was a new social studies teacher and a girl named Lena. The social studies teacher was a fat young woman with short hair. She had powdery skin and wore a lot of makeup. She was gripping Lena's blouse, pushing her out of the room. Lena let herself be forced into the hall, then snatched a fistful of the teacher's blouse. They froze, glaring hatefully into each other's narrowed eyes. The class erupted into the hall.

"Let go," the teacher breathed.

Lena hung on.

"Let go," the woman hissed. She was breathing hard.

They clung to each other and started to circle. I was the only other adult around. I took Lena's arms firmly but gently. "Easy, Lena," I said, "easy."

"Get your hands *off* me," the teacher shrieked suddenly. Tears swelled in her blank, blue eyes. Lena's fingers spread. I drew her back. The assistant principal arrived. He took Lena's arm and led her away.

The teacher's fat white face struggled against the sobs that were beginning to shake her. Lena glanced over her shoulder. She was smiling faintly.

"You pig," the teacher sobbed. "Oh, goddamn you." She slapped her plump hands to her face and started down the steps after Lena and the assistant principal. "You finally brought me down to your level, goddamn you."

During my own school days the worst thing I had

seen was a kid who swore at a teacher. He had stood up by his desk and said, "Aw, go to hell." The teacher had told him to get out, but he was out the door already. Later he apologized. The teacher let him back into the class for that.

Leon Stuart had come to us from one of the State's halfway houses. These were homes for boys, that stood on the divide between prison and polite society. The boys were sent to the halfway houses when they were judged almost cured. They lived in attractive, cheery houses with ten or eleven other boys, supervised by strict but kind adults. They got jobs and went to school. Later, some of them went home.

Leon was a scrawny, slouching kid with large buck teeth. Before he entered a room, he would slip his head through the doorway and glance into every corner, the way a cat does when you let him out. He had done a lot of breaking and entering before the law got him. He hated school and skipped most of his classes, and I saw him in the library so much that we got to be good friends.

One time he came up while I was giving a lesson on the comma. I was perched on top of a table and Taylor Smith and three others were sitting around another table. Leon sloped in and stood over them. He was wearing a purple shirt and purple slacks.

"Tut," I was saying, "give me a sentence with a comma."

Tut was a sleepy-looking kid who played in a neighborhood soul band. His eyes rolled up toward Leon. "Leon stole some paper out of Taylor's notebook, *comma,* but he didn't get away with it." Everyone laughed.

"Very good," I said.

"What you talkin about?" Leon said.

"Taylor, another sentence with a comma," I said.

"Leon's fingers is light, *comma,* but he don't have no brains to go with it." More laughter. Leon couldn't help smiling.

"Roosevelt," I said.

"The next time Leon steals paper, *comma,* we gonna kick his butt."

I couldn't keep from laughing any more. The librarian glared at us from the other end of the room.

"Can I do one?" Leon asked.

"Sure," I said.

"Taylor, *comma,* Tut, *comma,* Roosevelt, *comma,* is all, *comma,* punks, *comma.*"

"No good," I said.

"What you mean?"

"Too many commas."

One day Leon asked me if I wanted to come over to the house and play football with the boys.

"Sure," I said.

I went straight home after school and pulled on blue jeans, a sweatshirt, and sneakers, and bounced out into the yellow November afternoon. It was warm, and the burnt leaf smell of autumn was in the air. I sprinted against a red light on Hamilton and jogged down Burlingame to the halfway house. It was a big brick house near Woodward Avenue. I rang the doorbell. Leon opened the door.

"What's happenin, Mr. Hough?" he said merrily, and led me through the living room to an office in back. A black man with a tough, intelligent face was sitting at a desk.

"This is Mr. Harris," Leon said. We shook hands.

Leon scampered off to round up the kids. "This is nice of you," Mr. Harris said.

"I love to play," I said.

"Well, you really found someone to play with," he said.

There were six of them. Three were big boys with mustaches and stiff, suspicious faces. One of them was named Charlie. He was built like Michelangelo's David, with thicker shoulders. He had lost one of his front teeth, and he spat through the gap. There were three smaller boys, about Leon's size.

We marched south on Woodward to an empty lot next to the gray cathedral. It was a big lot, all humps and bowls, littered with rocks as big as your fist.

We filed out onto the middle of the field. The sun was setting. It was chilly. "Tackle or touch?" I asked. I thought that since there were seven of us, I would be quarterback for each team. I figured I could always get rid of the ball before any of these kids could get me. I had been an all-conference guard in high school, and an end for a small college team. "Tackle or touch?"

"What the fuck you think?"growled Charlie.

I glanced at the field. It was hard and stony.

Charlie spotted a kid in a long black coat walking along Woodward Avenue. He jogged over to him, and they chatted. I sat down and waited. The kid came back with Charlie.

"I'm playin," he announced. He was tall and thin, with a studious face. "I'll pick up against Charlie," he said, peeling off his coat. He was wearing pressed green slacks and black pointed shoes.

Charlie chose first and took Lee, a big glowering kid who hadn't said anything since I'd been there. The new kid ran his eyes up and down my arms and legs.

"Are you bad?"

I shrugged.

"No, man. Be honest. Are you bad, or what?"

"I'm all right," I said.

"Then I'll take you, baby."

Charlie took the other big kid, so we inherited two of the small boys.

The new kid introduced himself. His name was Dixon and he had been a third-string quarterback at Northern High School.

They kicked off to us. Dixon snatched the ball on the second bounce and sprinted. Charlie and Lee caught him at the same time; Charlie drove a shoulder into his belly and Lee grabbed his neck, and they flattened him.

On our first play I ran a quick square-out and Dixon threw the ball to me. In an instant Charlie had me around the chest. His arms felt like chunks of iron. He held me for a few seconds, making sure of his grip, then hurled me to the ground. I hit as though I had fallen two stories. That ground would have had to be asphalt to be any harder than it was.

They tackled like street fighters. The smaller ones were afraid to get tackled, but now and then we persuaded one to run with the ball. Then Charlie or Lee would catch him and toss him like a rag doll. Once I bent over the ball to center it, and Lee stood over me and rammed me so hard I flipped onto my back.

The game was close. We traded touchdown for touchdown. Dixon threw a lot of passes to me, and I caught them and rolled with the tackles.

"Let's try a long one," Dixon whispered in the huddle late in the game. "Fake that short one and go long."

Ten yards away Charlie waited for me. I took off, pretended to stop in front of him, and as he lunged I danced around him and turned on all my speed. Dixon's pass rose like a balloon. *Oh, Christ.* I had to stop and wait for it. I could hear Charlie running. The ball seemed suspended up there. I jumped, caught it on the tips of my fingers, and the ground hit me like a speeding truck. Everything disappeared and I thought I was knocked out, but consciousness popped back and my mid-section felt like jelly. It was as though everything had been squeezed out of my stomach. I made myself get up and staggered to the huddle. Charlie was watching me. I bent over casually and picked a blade of dry grass and stuck it in my mouth. I thought I might be sick.

It was getting dark. The score was tied. We had the ball and a chance to win.

"Let's try another long one," Dixon said.

Oh, Lord. "All right," I said. "We'll try it, but for Christ sake don't hang it up there. I almost got killed last time."

"I'm hip," he said.

Charlie went for the fake again, and I ran away from him. This time Dixon really threw the ball. It cleared Charlie by plenty. I caught it in stride and pranced across the goal line.

Dixon scurried over, yelling, "My boy, my boy," and gave me both palms to slap. We had won. Pain filled my belly like an awful meal. We walked slowly back along Woodward as the sun fell out of sight, and I left them at the halfway house.

Charlie jogged up the steps and paused on the porch. "Hey," he said. I peered at him. It was getting dark. "That was a pretty good tackle, wasn't it?"

"Yeah," I said. "It wasn't bad at all." It hurt to talk. I thought my ribs must be broken.

It hurt so much I couldn't sleep, and next day I went to Metropolitan Hospital. They x-rayed my ribs. Nothing was broken but they told me I'd torn the muscle away from the rib cage. They gave me pills for the pain and told me to come back if it hurt after five days, for that might mean a ruptured spleen. But it went away.

"How'd you like the game?" Leon asked me cheerfully the next day.

"Great," I said.

"We got to play again sometime."

"Sure," I said. "You bet."

Taylor Smith and Tut, bundled in long black coats, followed me out of the library. Robert Simmons was in the hall, gazing out the window. I hadn't seen Robert for a week. I had been looking for him. We were just getting to know each other then.

"Where you all goin?" he said.

"We're going to the museum."

Robert's hands were rammed deep into his coat pockets. He looked at me as though I'd asked him to enroll in dancing school.

"I don't want to go to no museum."

"Then go home," I said.

"If I go home, the police gonna be lookin for me." He came to school very seldom, and a truant officer had been after him.

"Well, we're going to the museum," I said.

Robert peered out the window. "I guess I got to go," he said.

We picked up Leotis downstairs. He was hiding out in

the boys' room, and he spotted us and darted out. "Where you all goin?"

"To the museum."

"Let me come with you, man."

"You're supposed to be in class," I said. "I can't take you."

"Come on, man." He was walking with us.

I shrugged. "I guess you can go."

I got bus tickets in the office and we walked out into the bright chilly air on Twelfth Street. We were going to take the Davison bus to Woodward and the Woodward bus all the way to the Cultural Center.

"Hey, Mr. Hough," Robert said. "Hey, let me get my brother's car."

"What for?" I said. "We got free bus tickets."

"I don't want to take no bus," he said.

I stopped. "Why not?"

"There might be someone I know on the bus. There might be a girl I know. They expect me to be ridin in a car, man."

"Lord, Robert," I said.

"Forget it," he said.

They sat in the bus like watchful spiders, wrapped tightly in their black coats. The bus lurched down Woodward and let us out in front of the Detroit Public Library. The Cultural Center nestled in the middle of the complex of Wayne State University. The white stone library stared across Woodward at the Art Institute, and the Historical Museum sat off to the side, a smaller partner. I shepherded them into the Historical Museum.

We made a systematic tour. The old automobiles fascinated them. Robert stood apart, hands in pockets, and when he spoke the others listened. Sometimes they argued, but Robert's husky voice cut through theirs and ended it. Taylor seemed most ready to try to learn something. Tut chattered. Leotis smiled insolently. We saw reconstructed Colonial rooms, uniforms of the Revolutionary War, model ships.

The sky had gone gray and a cold wind was sweeping Woodward Avenue when we came out of the museum. It was past noon. We walked south, past the library, and turned into a dirty, over-heated diner near Warren Avenue.

The boys sat at a table against the wall, and I sat at the counter where I could swivel on my stool and watch them. Taylor and Tut had money and said they could buy their lunch; I said I would buy a hamburger and coke for Robert and Leotis. I watched them eat. Tut rattled on, his voice rising and falling musically, his eyes smiling. Now and then Taylor broke into his glorious grin. Leotis hunched over his food, smiling ironically. Robert ate silently, as though he were thinking about things that were beyond them, but he smiled faintly at Tut. I watched them as I ate. They had been real gentleman in the museum. I sipped my coffee. It tasted fine.

They finished and sauntered to the door. I gulped the last of my coffee and took my check to the cash register beside the door. A fat white woman was perched on a stool behind the cash register.

"I'm paying for three," I said. "Two have paid."

"No," she said. "One paid."

The red and white keys of the cash register were giggling at me. I had been double-crossed. "I'll be right back," I said. I darted out.

The wind was blowing hard and the first snowflakes of the year rode it down Woodward. I spotted Taylor across Warren Avenue. I knew who hadn't paid.

"You tell Tut to get over here," I yelled to Taylor through the wind and the whirling snowflakes. Taylor opened the door to a drugstore and a moment later Tut came out, grinning. He crossed the street and I grabbed him by the arm and swung him through the door of the diner. The woman sat up there on her stool like a judge. Tut passed his check and money to her.

"In here we pay for what we eat, young man," she said.

"Yes, mam," Tut said.

I paid my bill and told the woman I was sorry. She shrugged. She wouldn't look at me.

Outside I went after Tut. "Look," I said. "I don't care what you do on your own. But when you're with me, I'm responsible for what you do. It's my fault that you didn't pay." I looked at Robert for help. "Am I right, Robert?"

Robert and Taylor and Leotis stood a little apart and stared at the sidewalk.

"Am I right, Robert?"

"But Mr. Hough," he said. He spoke apologetically, as though it hurt him to have to disillusion me. "Dig. When you think you can get away with somethin, you got to try. You just got to."

I looked away, across the street to the white façade of the Art Institute. *When you think you can get away with somethin, you got to try.* When I was a kid, shoplifting in the five-and-ten was a luxury enjoyed by some of the more naughty boys. But stealing wasn't always a luxury around Twelfth Street. Sometimes kids like Tut and Robert had to steal to eat right. Life didn't hand them as much as it had handed me. They had to try to get away with things.

I was the quietest of all on the bus back to Twelfth Street.

"It's time you got into some kind of social life," Larry Phillips, the librarian, told me. Larry lived out in Oak Park with his parents. He was trim and athletic. Cheerfully, competently, he put books into the hands of the children. But he didn't really know — or wouldn't admit — what the children needed most. If he had, he would have replaced some of those knights and heroes on his walls with Malcolm X and Martin Luther King.

"It sure is," I said.

So he introduced me to a girl named Beth, a lab assistant to a biologist at the University of Michigan. She lived in Livonia. She was a petite girl with short brown

84

hair and a stiff, sunburned face. She had grown up near Boston, and gone to Boston University.

Larry arranged a blind date, and we went to a movie with him and his girl friend. He drove a sports car. Beth and I sat in the back seat, and I smelled a woman's perfume in the dark for the first time since I had come into Vista.

It was two days after the Tigers had won the World Series, and everyone was still buzzing about it.

"I won five dollars," I said.

"I won ten," Beth said.

Larry snorted. "You didn't know what you were doing."

"Yeah, I knew what I was doing," Beth said. "I knew Gibson couldn't beat the Tigers three times."

"Hey," I said. "That's just how I figured it." I looked at her. I don't know where she got her red-brown color in October.

After the movie Larry said we were going to the best place in town, and he drove us to a bar out on Seven Mile Road called the Trade Winds. The entertainer was a young black man named Bill, who played the guitar and sounded like a cross between Sam Cooke and Tom Jones. After Bill's first set Larry introduced him to Beth and me. Larry seemed to know him well. He was a fine-looking man, built like a welterweight boxer and dressed in a sparkling white Nehru jacket. The Trade Winds was dark and low-ceilinged, decorated with palm fronds and relics of the South Seas. Bill straddled a stool with his guitar on his knee in a very bright light behind the bar. Beth and I were drinking beer. My mother likes it, and perhaps for this reason I have always considered the taste for beer in women a sign of wholesomeness and of appreciation for the fundamentals. Larry sat across from us and poured his philosophies on teaching into his girl's ear.

"You must be an old Red Sox fan, growing up around Boston," I said.

"Listen," Beth said. "I can remember seeing Ted Williams." The soft light made her hair look fine and auburn.

"I can too," I said. "You remember Jackie Jensen?"

"Jensen, Piersall, and Williams. The best outfield in baseball."

"You remember Ike Delock?"

"Sore arm and all."

"Jesus," I said.

How often do you meet a girl like that? It took me back to the summers when I was ten and eleven, when my mother and father and I would get in the car on a Saturday morning and drive to Boston for a ball game. We would get there an hour before the game started and stand in the shadows at the back of the grandstand behind home plate and watch batting practice. My parents would drink beer and I would have a Coke. It smelled of beer and cigars up there on the cool, dark concrete ramp. We would watch them hit those high, arcing pellets that fell all over the bright outfield. It would be late when we got home and the sky would be clear and full of stars. You could smell the grass and the honeysuckle on the fence. All that seemed separated from Detroit not only by years and space, but by some dimension even more final. Talking to Beth about those old names brought it all back.

Late that night at the door to her apartment I asked her if I could see her again. She said yes.

Larry Phillips drove me back to the ghetto. "Thanks," I said. "Thanks, thanks, thanks." He smiled, feigning nonchalance, as though he had intervened to save me from a fine for speeding and didn't want to take the credit.

Webb Avenue was deserted. The big streetlamps and the neon lights of the gas station cast yellow pools on the sidewalk. I scurried inside. A cockroach slanted down the refrigerator door and disappeared underneath it when I flicked on the light. I didn't even try to get him.

One morning less than two weeks after I met Beth I woke up with a terrific fever. I called the school and told the secretary that I wouldn't be there, then I wrapped the blankets around my shoulders and plunged into a hot, damp sleep. It was late afternoon when I woke up. A gray half-light filled the room. The shut-in smell of gas was very strong. I drank some water and fell asleep again.

Next morning the fever had gone and I was very weak. I got up and opened the refrigerator. There was some hamburger and some frozen chicken pies. I telephoned Beth.

It was Saturday and she was home. "You sound awful," she said.

"I'm sick," I said. "Listen. I don't have anything good to eat."

"Wait right there," she said. I didn't have a chance to tell her to keep the car doors locked and to park close to my apartment.

I was asleep when she knocked on the door. She had come all the way from Livonia. Her arms were loaded with groceries. She was wearing slacks and a white shirt, and her face was ruddy and glowing above the starched linen.

I got back into bed and she went into the kitchen. I heard her slapping cans down on the table and rattling pans, and pretty soon she came out with a tall glass of orange juice and a bowl of soup. I sat up and drank it. She watched from the sofa. Then she took the plates out and I heard water running. I was lying on my back staring at the cracked ceiling when she came back. For a moment I felt like a wounded Hemingway hero. We talked a little. Beth was going to the indoor tennis courts at Wayne State University for a mixed doubles match. She played tennis every chance she got. She must have been very good. I had never played tennis.

"Can I see you Sunday night?" I asked.

"If you're well."

"I'll be well."

"All right."

I watched her click free the lock and slide out into the dusky hall. Next day I felt fine.

That night I took her out. She was the only person besides my mother who had ever taken care of me when I was sick. I took her to the most expensive place I could find, a nightclub high above the Detroit River. We had drinks made of pineapple juice and mango juice and gin. I couldn't have afforded many dates like that.

"You ought to come out and have dinner with me at least once a week," Beth said. She was on her second drink. The glass looked huge in her hands. "It's tough work you're doing." We danced, and she touched the back of my neck with the tips of her fingers.

Afterwards in her apartment I kissed her the way you do when you mean business. She kissed back, then tilted her head. "I think I'd better tell you something."

I let her go. I knew what she was going to say. "You're engaged," I said. I tried to sound casual.

"Not engaged," she said. "But there is someone." She dropped her eyes to the floor.

I sat down. There were copies of *Newsweek* and *Life* on the table by the sofa. Beth sat beside me and hugged her knees.

"I'm always getting into this," she said.

Something I needed was dissolving. "Who's the guy?" I said.

"I met him in Washington," she said. "I don't get to see him much."

"What does he do?" I picked up *Newsweek* and tried to find the movie reviews.

"You're not going to believe this," she said. She was still hugging her knees, gazing across the room. "He's a secret service agent."

"What?"

"Really."

There were some record albums on the floor. Ray Charles was on top. He was smiling a big, soulful smile.

"So your boyfriend is helping the country by guarding the President."

"That's right."

"That's what we need, more young men who will devote themselves to the secret service. That's nice. That's really beautiful." Beth's high color was suddenly deeper and redder. I didn't care what I said now. "Carries a gun. I bet he can really shoot it, too."

"Maybe so," she said.

"I bet he's a tough mother," I said.

"Stop it."

"Sure. I'll stop it."

"Look," she said. "I enjoy these evenings. I really do. But I just have to let you know how it is."

"Thanks," I said.

I went home. As I was climbing the steps four rapid cracks barked somewhere behind the apartment building. Gunshots. The silence returned. I paused in the doorway. A car swept past on Hamilton Street. Someone slammed a door in the hall upstairs.

The radiator in my apartment sizzled noisily, filling the room with its unwholesome heat. I opened the window. As I was getting into bed voices passed in the alley outside.

"She's fine."

"I know she is, brother, but you fuck with her and her old man gonna jump on you."

"That's all right. I might be waitin for him."

The voices trailed off and died, and I fell asleep listening to the radiator sizzle and hiss in the empty darkness.

FOUR

LITTLE JAMIE was sitting in the office along the wall where the bad boys waited for the principal. He was sitting there with his wrists on his knees, staring at the floor. You could tell that he had been through this many times.

"Hey," I said, and knelt in front of him. My eyes were level with his. I had seen him around. He was a very small fourth-grader. But you noticed him. He had the face of an old man, and alert brown eyes with crow's feet; and he smiled out of the corner of his mouth. His skin didn't have the usual chocolate sheen; it was tinged with gray. It was the gray of the sidewalks and gutters, and Jamie seemed to have picked it up, as though he had been rolling in it.

"What's the matter?" I said. His brown eyes focused on me, looking me over. "What happened?"

"Oh, he won't talk." I looked over my shoulder. It was the elementary school principal. She was an old woman with a powdered white face and bright red lipstick. She stood with her hands on her skinny hips and glared at Jamie. His eyes climbed over my shoulder and leaped at her like darts.

"Sure he will," I said. "He'll talk to me."

"If you can get him to talk to you, you'll be the first one," she said. She watched Jamie as though he had the measles and she had told him not to. I waited till she was gone.

"Come on, now," I said. "What happened?"

He tilted back his head and stared at the ceiling, as though he'd been told to spell a word for the hundredth time. "Miz Rogers, that history teacher," he began. "She talkin about I throwed a eraser. She say, 'Pick up that eraser.' I say, 'I didn't throw no eraser.' She always jumpin on me. She think I do everything that happens in that room."

The elementary school principal was above us again.

"James, if Mr. Hough takes you up to your class, will you calm down?" She had a snappy, high voice, like the yap of a poodle.

Jamie nodded without looking at her.

"All right," she said.

The history teacher, a black girl, opened the door and watched Jamie slink to his desk. His hands were stuffed in his pockets. Before he sat he glanced at the silent faces around him, daring them to speak. He lowered himself in behind the worn desktop. There were names and dirty words scribbled on it. Jamie let his head fall to his chest. His hands stayed in his pockets.

The history teacher went on with her lesson. She spoke aggressively, as though she were briefing them on survival and would only say it once. She was talking about Eskimos. She said they hunted caribou, which she wrote on the blackboard. It was an old blackboard, smoky with age and chalk dust. Jamie never looked up. I left him slumped like a tattered little sack, staring at the rickety desktop while his teacher revealed the existence of caribou and igloos and narwhals.

He lived with his mother and seven brothers in a decaying house between Twelfth Street and Woodrow Wilson. His mother was young. She worked in a printing shop and brought home seventy-five dollars a week. Jamie's father had moved out, but you still saw him around the neighborhood, a burly man with a mustache who was always drunk. One night he had shoved his way into the house, staggering and reeking beer, and the boys and their mother had wrestled him to the floor and thrown a bucket of cold water on him. Jamie laughed to tell about it.

It was a big empty house, as gray as Jamie's face. The paint was worn off the porch. The screen door hung from one hinge. The living room rug was gray, the sofa was gray, and the wallpaper had faded to gray-brown. In the next room a table leaned against the wall. A television sat on it like a fat pet. Beyond that was the kitchen. I never got to know more than two of Jamie's brothers. There were so many of them, and they were so close in age, that it was like trying to distinguish among a huge litter of kittens. Isaac was the oldest. He was fourteen. Jamie, eleven, was next, and then came Nathaniel. After that they blended into a squirming, crawling litter that surrounded me with gaping round faces whenever I walked into that living room. They wore filthy shorts and filthy t-shirts. Their mother was away from seven in the morning till five in the afternoon.

Jamie stayed out on the streets until one or two in the morning. He was growing up in the jungle. He was agile and speedy. He knew how to stand back in the shadows on the other side of the street. He knew how to keep his mouth shut. Like a highly evolved little animal, he could cope with his environment.

I took Jamie as a student at the start of the second semester. Erlinda and I had moved out of the library to the elementary reading room, where a woman named Mrs. Brooks taught. Mrs. Brooks was about thirty-five. She taught reading during the school year, Head Start in the summer. She spoke to each child in an earnest, motherly tone that seemed to acknowledge all the sadness in his life. The children trusted her. She worked with groups of elementary schoolers around long tables.

It was a colorful room, with big red and blue letters hung all over the walls, words printed in rainbow pastels on the blackboard. Mrs. Brooks had the children leaf through magazines and cut out words they recognized and paste them on colored construction paper. These compositions, which the kids loved doing, were taped everywhere. They had chosen words like *life, cool, police, now, bad,* and *city.*

Jamie could read almost nothing. The first time we

sat down we read a book he had chosen. It was first or second grade level. Jamie peered into it.

"You read it," he said.

"No, go ahead," I said.

"I can do it," he said. "I just don't feel like readin."

"All right." I read a few words. There were two or three sentences on each page. Jamie watched. He knew a lot of the words.

"Okay," he said. "I'll read."

He knew about two thirds of the second grade words. I told him all he didn't know that first day. We read for half an hour, then walked down the empty hall to the boys' room. Jamie dug into his blue jean pocket and pulled out three pieces of candy. He ate one and gave two to me.

We read together every day that semester. I made a list of everything he finished and taped it to the wall in Mrs. Brooks's room. As the list grew, titles changed from things like *Where the Wild Things Are* to *Meet the American Indians* to *King Arthur*. He wanted to read now. When I tried to show him how to sound out a word, he would study the syllables as though they were about to move. They must have looked to him the way Greek did to me. He had seen it from time to time but never studied it. Sometimes he would bolt out of his seat, shove his hands into his pockets, and snarl, "Just tell me the word, man." Then I would wait for him to take a deep breath, maybe pace a little, and sit down again. He'd figure out the word.

Jamie was ready to fight anyone. Size or reputation meant nothing to him. He punched an elementary school teacher in the jaw one time. He punched the art teacher in the stomach. All it took to make him fight was an intrusion on what he thought were his rights.

One time I found him along the wall in the office glaring back into the eyes of the elementary school principal.

"I don't know what to do with you, James," she was saying.

He was slumped back in the little chair, glowering sideways at her. His tattered sneakers were the color of the sidewalks they lived on. The pocket of his flannel shirt was torn away.

"Will you take him up to Mr. Ford's room?" the principal asked me. Mr. Ford was Jamie's teacher.

"Come on, Jamie," I said.

He whirled off the chair, brushing the principal, and hurled himself into the hall. He was squeezing a note she had written to Mr. Ford, and he crumpled it and flung it against the wall. He stuck his hands in his pockets and walked quickly away from me.

I caught him. He was sobbing. "I ain't goin to Mr. Ford's room," he hissed. "She want to do me like that. She always want to do me like that." He shut his eyes against the tears, but some of them were getting out. I nudged him into the empty corridor to the auditorium and held him. He tried to squirm away. I held him. His little body went slack.

"Come on," I said. "Let's go up to Mrs. Brooks's room. You don't have to go to Mr. Ford's room."

One day he was playing one of Mrs. Brooks's word games with a junior high student of mine named Melvin, a kid who was a couple of inches taller than I. The game was like Parchesi, but every time you landed you had to read a word and think of another that began the same way. Jamie and Melvin bet a quarter on the game. Jamie said he won. Melvin said Jamie had cheated. I got there just as the argument was turning into something. Jamie was standing ten feet from Melvin.

"You gonna pay me my quarter?"

Melvin sat there and grinned.

"Well, you get up then," Jamie said.

Melvin grinned. "Boy, I'll take you and flush you down the toilet," he said, and laughed. He wore nicely pressed red pants. Some of my other junior high students were standing around watching it.

"Come on and try it then," Jamie said in his little boy's tenor. He stepped up and slugged Melvin on the upper arm. Melvin laughed and stood up. Jamie cocked his fist and fired it as high on Melvin's chest as he could reach. I pulled him away before Melvin's patience wore out.

Jamie's longest feud was with a boy his own age named Derrick. Even Derrick was bigger than Jamie. Derrick was square and husky, with a bull neck. I don't know how the war began. In the same room they were like coral fish in the same tank. There would be ritualistic cockings of heads or kicks under a table, dirty words, and a flurry of hard little fists.

One day Jamie and Derrick were sitting with a group around the low table playing the word game. I didn't expect a fight. After the last one I had talked to Jamie, sitting on the window ledge in the hall. "It doesn't make sense to fight him," I had said. "Now I'm going to ask you as a favor to me to forget Derrick. Just forget him. Ignore him." Jamie nodded and we hopped down off the window ledge.

Mrs. Brooks was standing over the table watching the game. I was across the room with Walter and Gene, two of my boys.

Derrick made the usual challenges. "You cheatin, Jamie," he kept saying. Jamie didn't look at Derrick. He studied the game like a hustler dealing stud. "You cheatin, Jamie." Jamie kept his eyes on the board. Derrick quit talking and did something to Jamie under the table.

Jamie sprang up and kicked his chair away. Derrick launched himself out of his seat and Jamie hit him twice before he was erect. Derrick kicked and Jamie dodged and grabbed his foot and yanked him onto his back. Mrs. Brooks was trying to pull Jamie away. I got over there and pressed him against the blackboard, and big Walter grabbed Derrick.

Derrick had lost control. Tears of rage ran down his heavy cheeks. He writhed on the floor, trying to plunge after Jamie. Walter held him. He had so much muscle in his neck and shoulders that Walter, who was my biggest boy, couldn't pin him. I kept Jamie with me.

"Derrick had better go to the office," Mrs. Brooks said. Walter and Gene dragged him to the door. Gene was a greasy fat kid. Suddenly Derrick whipped his arm around, jerking Gene to the floor. Gene swore. They dragged Derrick out.

I took Jamie's arm and led him down the hall to Mr. Ford's room.

"I don't want to go to Mr. Ford's room."

"I thought you promised me you wouldn't fight Derrick any more?" I said. Jamie turned as though at bay at the door to Mr. Ford's room. My hand was still on his shoulder, and he shook it off. He tilted his head.

"Just tell me one thing," he whispered. "You ever been in a fight? You ever once been in a fight?" I didn't answer. "You a damn sissy, that's what," he said.

The door opened and Mr. Ford stood there. He had a yardstick in his hand. He was a tall black man with a goatee and the kids were afraid of him. He liked to use that yardstick. He looked at Jamie and shook his head. Jamie shot one more glance at me and followed Mr. Ford into the room, swinging his shoulders.

Walter and Gene were waiting for me in Mrs. Brooks's room. "Little motherfucker's strong," Gene said.

"Did you get him to the office?" I asked.

"Sure."

"Thanks," I said. "Let's quit for today."

They snapped shut their books and went out. Mrs. Brooks was at the table with her kids. The fight hadn't made her angry. She had helped stop it almost apologetically. She was so attuned to the unhappiness of the children that I wondered about her own life. I went to the window and leaned on the shelf and stared out at the playground. The gym classes were still playing touch football. I watched the boys. A kid in pink pants and sneakers was sent straight down field for a pass. He sprinted under the ball, looking back over his shoulder, and plowed into the defender. The defender was smaller. He wore glasses. He spun and his glasses sailed as though they had been thrown off a merry-go-round. The receiver stopped and the defender got up and punched him on the jaw. They started hitting and kicking and clawing, and as the crowd clustered around, the burly gym teacher jogged over and got between them. *You a damn sissy.* They were cursing each other and pointing with their index fingers. *You a damn sissy.* I turned away from the window. The bell jangled. School was out.

The room emptied. I sat on top of Mrs. Brooks's desk and stared at the clock on the top of the Sears Building. Mrs. Brooks was picking up pencils.

"What's the matter?" she said.

"Nothing anyone can do anything about," I said.

A week after I had arrived in Detroit I crossed Twelfth Street in the middle of the afternoon and found a gang clustered around the school door. I kept my eyes on the sidewalk and pushed through them. No one said anything. I climbed the steps and grabbed the bar to pull open the door.

"Hey, motherfucker."

I froze with my hand on the door.

"Talkin to you, motherfucker."

I looked back. There was a car at the curb. It was full. A kid with a chipped tooth was talking to me from the passenger's seat in front. Everyone else was watching me. All I had to do was yank open the door and disappear, but I stood on the top step and stared at him.

"Who you lookin at, baby?" He pushed open the car door and stood up. He was wearing a dungaree jacket. "Hey, motherfucker, you want me?"

I shook my head slowly. No sir, I didn't want him. He leaned on the car door. He smiled. I walked into the building.

Late one afternoon I was crossing Hamilton near my apartment. The city was emptying. The cars hunched bumper to bumper in a line at the red light at Hamilton and Webb. A tall kid in yellow slacks was standing in the middle of the stalled traffic. Something had happened before I got there. The kid was peering into the window of a white station wagon. It was full of white people.

"Hey!" he yelled at the shut window. He grabbed the door handle, but the door was locked.

"Pull him out of the car, Leroy!" Three more kids were knifing through the traffic. They surrounded the car and snatched at the locked door handles. They hammered with their fists on the roof. I could see the face of the white man in the driver's seat. He was smoking a pipe. He looked like a philosophy professor. He stared straight ahead, biting the pipe, his face tight and pale. The light turned green and the cars began to inch forward. The station wagon crept ahead. The kids banged on its side and one of them spat on the window. Then the line untangled and the station wagon jumped clear and spun off. I watched from the storefront church on the corner of Hamilton and Webb. I wondered how it had started. If any of them had spotted me, I would have run.

Mrs. Brooks patted my arm. "You're doing a good job," she said.

"Sure," I said. I took my jacket off its hook in the closet and slung it over my shoulder.

Jamie was leaning against the wall out in the hall. He wasn't looking at me. I walked down the stairs and out onto Twelfth Street. I looked down. Jamie was walking beside me.

"I'll walk you home," he said.

We didn't talk. Smells hung in the thick air along

Woodrow Wilson. There was garbage, beer, exhaust fumes, and the smoky, cindery smell of the city. My head felt sealed off from it all. I walked home half-unconscious.

Jamie followed me down the damp cool hall to my apartment door. I rattled the lock and let him in.

"Get some oranges," I said.

I pulled off my necktie. Jamie found two oranges in the refrigerator and sat down on the big bed and started to peel his. I put an Aretha Franklin record on my stereo and dropped down beside Jamie. Aretha sang "Think." We stripped the oranges.

"Hey, I just remembered," Jamie said. He stretched so he could reach into his pocket and pulled out some candy. He had six pieces. We split them. Aretha was singing "I Say a Little Prayer for You." I unwrapped a piece of candy.

"Want to go down to the Fisher Building?" I said. Jamie loved its marble floors and the display windows of its shops.

"I ain't got no bus fare," he said.

"That's all right," I said. "I got it."

"Let's go then," he said.

All my boys had been like Jamie. They took it until they were fifteen. Then they were ready to leave school. Suddenly they were too big and too tough to have to give in to teachers. Sometimes they hit one. Then they were expelled and sent to special schools or to boys' homes. Sometimes they just stopped going to classes. Sometimes they walked out for good. They gave up on school because knowing algebra and adjectives and American history didn't help them in their broken homes and on the streets that seemed to stretch endlessly on every side of them.

But it was hard to forget school. I knew many who had been expelled. They kept coming back. They sneaked into the building and wandered up and down the halls. They mingled with the students changing classes. They hung around my students in the library and in Mrs. Brooks's room. It was a risk. The assistant principal was always looking for them, and sometimes the principal called the police.

After Taylor Smith's brother Rick attacked the teacher with the map rack he was sent to a boys' home. A few months later he ran away and went to live with friends. The police couldn't find him. He started coming to school.

I didn't know him. But I'd heard. A glimpse of him in the hall sent teachers scurrying to the principal. Some even threatened to quit if Rick Smith wasn't kept out of the building. So I wasn't glad the first time he sauntered into Mrs. Brooks's room. I pretended not to notice him. He sat in a corner and began to talk to a couple of girls. The girls liked him. He was lean and hard and he had a reputation. I kept an eye on him. After all the stories about him, I expected anything. He stayed several hours. Next day he came back. We talked.

"Every teacher in this school is scared of you," I told him.

"I ain't that bad," he said.

"I know you're not," I said.

I found time to chat with him. He was living with friends in a tenement building on a side street off Davison. He didn't want to go back to the boys' home. Sometimes he sat with my students and listened to me teach. He never interrupted or played around. He came almost every day.

He started bringing friends. There was a kid named Freddy who had been thrown out of Central High School. He and Rick roamed the halls, and teachers spotted them. Several times they had to run. Once Rick was in the library with me and the assistant principal stepped in and glanced around. Rick jumped up. "Turn and pretend you're looking for a book," I whispered. He spun and faced the shelves, and the assistant principal's scrutiny slid over him.

After a month of hiding out, Rick decided to surrender and go back to the boys' home. He went home and his mother called the probation officer. The day he was to go back, he came to see me.

"What's the name and address of this place?" I asked.

He gave them to me.

"I'll call you up. Maybe we can go out to a movie or something," I said.

"That'd be all right," he said.

"I hope everything goes all right."

"I just decided to get it over with," he said. He glanced up at the clock. "I got to slide on." His voice was soft and deep. "I got to be there at two."

"Good luck."

I called the home several times, but they wouldn't let me take him out. He stayed there a month, then I started seeing him again. He was skipping classes. Finally he ran away again. The last thing I heard he was in jail. He and a friend had robbed a store and nearly collided with a Tactical Mobile Unit cruiser on their way out. They had run into an alley and the cops had started shooting. Rick and his buddy knew enough to stop right there. Rick had a long juvenile record, and he was going to serve some time now.

Another who couldn't stay away was Leotis, who had gone with me to the historical museum. Leotis had been expelled about the time Rick had been. Leotis was a gangling kid with toothpick arms and legs. He looked like a spider. He had a cheerful, gap-toothed smile. The principal couldn't stand him.

Leotis used to come up and talk to the girls or sit around while I taught. One afternoon I was sitting in Mrs. Brooks's room with little Jamie and Taylor Smith, and Leotis drifted in and pulled up a chair. He was wearing a brown leather jacket and carrying a black hat. He sat down and stretched his long legs under the table.

"What's happenin?" he grinned.

The principal walked in. There were pools of pink on

his face. "I'm looking for a boy in a brown leather jacket," he said. He focused on Leotis. "Ah, yes." A huge black policeman clanked in. He was a motorcycle cop in a heavy dark-blue jacket and helmet. His gun and handcuffs dangled from his belt. Leotis got up and the cop grabbed him and shoved him out of the room.

The principal looked at me. "I wish you'd tell me when these boys come around," he said.

"Sure."

And Leotis came back. One morning he ducked in and asked me to keep his coat for him. He would be less conspicuous without a coat.

"Lord," I said. "What's going to happen to me if they find out I'm holding your coat? I'm supposed to throw you out of the building."

"Come on, man," Leotis smiled. "You my man, ain't you?"

"I'll tell you what," I said. "The closet is over there. Why don't you put your coat in the closet without telling me."

He came back for his coat when the three o'clock bell rang.

The last day I saw him I was at the window in the hall. Out on the street Leotis strolled into view. A motorcycle cop was leading him by the arm. It looked like the same cop that had taken him out of the library that day. I got to the office at the same time that Leotis and the policeman did. Leotis nodded to me. There was a kid sitting holding a wet wad of paper towel against his face. One of his eyes was swollen almost shut and a secretary was on her hands and knees at his feet wiping the floor with a wet rag. She stood up. There was a big slick spot where she had wiped.

The kid on the chair glowered at Leotis.

"What happened?" the principal said.

"He pulled a knife on me," Leotis said.

"I didn't!" The kid shot up, clutching the wet paper towel to his bleeding face.

"All right, all right," the principal said. "You sit down."

Leotis shrugged and sat down beside his enemy. The policeman leaned on the counter and the principal went to the telephone.

"We're going to put a stop to this," he said.

I never saw Leotis again.

Another who kept coming was Nathan. Nathan was a dwarf with processed hair. He had been expelled early in the year, and after a long absence he started coming to Mrs. Brooks's room.

"Nathan Burgess has been coming into the building," the principal said to me one day. He knew that Nathan had been hanging around me and my boys, but he didn't want to accuse me. The principal hated confrontations. "If you see him, put him out, will you?"

The same day Nathan showed up. He settled in a corner of Mrs. Brooks's room and chatted with some girls. I was working with Jamie and Mrs. Brooks was holding up flash cards for a group of her little ones. It was incredible the way she let my kids walk in and out of her room. No one else in the school would have tolerated them. Nathan stayed in the corner and talked quietly. If he hadn't been in that room, he would have been out on the street. I wasn't going to throw him out. If the principal came in, I decided I'd pretend I hadn't seen Nathan slip in.

A few hours later Nathan and Taylor headed down the stairs toward the door. Taylor had his hand on the knob when the art teacher waddled around the corner. She faced them with her hands on her hips.

"Where do you think you two are going?"

All Taylor had to do was explain that he was my student and had permission to leave early. But the art teacher stood in their way like a military policeman and asked them again, "Just where do you think you're going?"

"We goin home, lady."

The art teacher dropped her thick hand on Nathan's shoulder. Even she was taller than he was. She started to haul him away from the door, and he spread his palm against her collar bone and shoved her. She floundered back and hit the steel lockers with a crash. Before Taylor and Nathan could get out, the big shop teacher was there. The shop teacher took Nathan's arm and led him down the hall to the office. The art teacher trotted beside them, her face scarlet.

"I'm gonna kick your ass, lady," Nathan said, pointing at her.

"You'll be in jail," the art teacher shouted. There were a lot of students in the hall. "How you going to kick my ass from jail?" the art teacher shouted. The kids stared at her.

Taylor had slipped away. He came back and told me what had happened. "Why don't you do somethin, Mr. Hough?"

"What can I do?"

"They gonna take Nathan down to the Tenth Precinct. Tell 'em he wasn't doin nothin."

"Taylor, I can't. He's been warned a hundred times to stay out of the building. I wasn't even supposed to let him in here."

Taylor's eyes were slitted and his lips were pursed.

"Why didn't you just tell her the truth?" I said. "It would have been so easy. I know some teachers don't act right, but all you had to do then was explain you had permission to leave."

Taylor stared past me. "She didn't have no right grabbin Nathan."

"Yeah, but where did it get you?" I asked.

"She didn't have no right grabbin Nathan."

Every day at three from September to June a crowd collected at the school doors. It was hard to reckon ages, but they all must have been under twenty. Rick was almost always there, and Leotis, until they took him away. Nathan turned up again. It was a baleful, hostile crowd, mostly male. They smoked cigarettes and chewed gum. Not all of them were waiting for girl friends. The bell would ring and the kids would gush out. Some would knife through the crowd and go home. Others stayed and swelled it. Kids on the street would hand cigarettes to those who had just come out, and they would fragment into clusters and smoke and talk. Then there would be a drifting away. Alone or in groups they would fan out and scatter across the empty lot, and the neighborhood would swallow them. Tomorrow they would all be back, a tight half circle around the doors to the school.

The librarian had found some posters somewhere and tacked them up all over the school. They were white sheets with bold black letters. They said: *BOY. Drop out of school and that's what they'll call you all your life.* The *BOY* was alone on the top line in huge letters. To be called boy is one of the greatest insults of all. The police used it. My kids told me that on Woodward Avenue, where the black neighborhoods rub against the white, they had been called "boy" and "nigger" many times. They hadn't dropped out of school yet. They were giving it a final try. And people were still calling them "nigger." People were still calling them "boy."

By the time they were fifteen, some of them had given up. They were still hearing "boy." So they got their hands up and hit teachers back. They smashed windows and pulled fire alarms and sometimes at night shot a few holes in the school. But there must have been a little hope still. For they came back. They came back until the police dragged them down to the station on Livernois and booked them for trespassing or truancy. They came back until it was really impossible for them to come any more.

FIVE

It was the smallest gym I had ever seen. I had been down there a few times. The white brick walls were less than five feet from the edge of the basketball court. The floorboards were so worn and white they looked as though they had been sandpapered. There were windows covered with wire mesh high along one wall, and the late afternoon sun slanted weak yellow rays against the whitewashed brick.

I pushed through the door cautiously, like an uninvited guest at a ball. I was wearing sweatclothes and sneakers, clutching my shirt and pants and necktie to my chest. I blinked.

There were six kids in the gym. They had stripped to shorts and put on jerseys. They wore white wool socks or black stockings pulled up over their hard calves. Their pants were carefully folded over chairs at the side of the court. They were taking easy shots. Someone would get the ball, prance out several steps, and toss it up with a snap of the wrist. I sat down on a chair at the side. George Bucknell nodded to me.

That afternoon Larry Phillips, the librarian, had brought him into our reading room. George had come over from Central High School. He had lean, delicate arms and legs. Larry introduced us.

"George and his buddies want to play basketball," Larry said. "They have permission to use the gym, but they've got to have an adult there."

"Can I bring my sneakers and get a workout?" I asked.

"Sure," George said.

"All right," I had said. "I'll be there after school."

They began a game. They played half court, since there were only three on a team. The game was to twelve. They were fast and agile. They had good eyes. They played gracefully and silently, and soon their knotted black shoulders and flat bellies were slick with perspiration.

I sat on my hands, with my folded clothes on my lap. I had never played basketball on an organized team. I had played on winter afternoons in the old gym at Haverford, pick-up games to take the mind off Spenser and Milton and imminent exams. I was a bad dribbler and I couldn't use my left hand. I sat on my hands and watched them flick the ball in neat, daring patterns beneath the basket.

The game ended. They paused, breathing deeply. George squinted at me. "Come on, Mr. Hough." The losers were drifting off the floor. I was supposed to choose two of them. I chose George and told him to pick the other.

I played cautiously. I felt that they were being polite

to me, like a good host who ignores the bad manners of a guest. I was a little wooden, but I scored some points and when we broke up at five thirty I had nothing to be embarrassed about.

"Can you come on Wednesday?" George said, as I switched off the lights. The gym was open every Monday and Wednesday.

"Be glad to," I said.

More than twenty kids flooded the gym on Wednesday. The word had spread. They were tall kids, already men. Some just stood on the sidelines and heckled the ballplayers. I spent most of the afternoon in the hall outside the gym watching for anyone who tried to get into the teachers' lounge or up the stairs.

Next day the principal called me to his office. "If you want to play basketball," he said, "you're going to have to cut down on the number of boys. The janitor told me you had more than twenty in there yesterday."

"I didn't expect so many," I said.

"They left cigarette butts on the gym floor."

"I didn't know they were smoking," I said. It must have been those smart ones on the sidelines.

"So you're going to have to do something," he concluded. "I don't know what, but something."

I made a telephone call to Central High School and asked the secretary to tell George to come see me. "I'll be honest," I said to him. "I can't throw ten of those big kids out if they don't want to go. Mr. Davidson's going to put an end to the whole thing if this happens again."

George nodded calmly. He had a small face, intelligent and patient. "We'll take care of it," he said.

"You think you can?"

"Don't worry."

We never had too many again. Now and then an outsider would try to get in. The game would stop and ten sweating, half-naked giants would take a menacing step and say, "Pull up, baby." The intruder would smile tightly and slink away. Sometimes a new boy came in and George would catch my eye and say, "He's cool." And he always was.

The first fight was between George and Jeffrey Glass. Jeffrey was wide-shouldered and very handsome. He was guarding George, and they began shoving and colliding. It was a close game. Their faces were tense with concentration. Suddenly Jeffrey pushed George too hard, and George whirled and flung the ball at him. Jeffrey took it against his shoulder and charged. They stood almost on top of each other and fired wild punches that smacked against their hard, dripping bodies. I got between them and wrapped my arms around George and drove him backward until I held him against the wall. Jeffrey tried to get him through me. I shouted to the others to grab him. Three of them pinned his arms. I pressed George against the wall. He glared over my shoulder at Jeffrey. His face was drenched. He took deep, angry breaths.

"I'll see you outside, motherfucker," Jeffrey hollered from across the room.

"Goddamn right you will," George called past my ear.

After the game I was sitting on the steps outside waiting for the librarian to give me a ride home. Jeffrey came out and sat down beside me.

"You all cooled down?" I asked.

"That wasn't nothin," he said. "We argue all the time."

Argue?

George popped out, buttoning his coat. Jeffrey got up and they started off across the parking lot toward the houses beyond. George looked back over his shoulder. "We argue all the time," he said.

Sometimes it lasted longer. George was in another fight with Jeffrey's brother Albert. Albert had a goatee and a lot of natural hair. They called him "Chip," because they thought he looked like a chipmunk when he smiled. He often clowned during the games, dribbling between his legs, taking absurd shots, or cavorting in front of the man he was guarding. But he would explode when his game was poor. The day he fought George he was missing shots. He started snapping elbows and bumping. George warned him.

"Why don't you do somethin about it?" Albert snarled.

They darted at each other, punching and kicking. It reminded me of a dogfight. I got between them and grabbed George. The punches kept flying. I caught one on the mouth. I felt the sting and taste of blood. I lowered my head and threw all my strength against George. He staggered back. The others stopped Albert.

George's tense body loosened. "It's all right, I'm cool now."

Albert wasn't in the gym. There was blood on the floor. I followed the spots out and into the teachers' lounge. Albert was standing in the middle of the room pressing a wet pad of paper towel to his face. Perspiration and blood mingled on his jaw.

"You all right?" I said.

He nodded and lowered the paper towel. The bleeding had stopped.

In the gym everyone was dressing. I grabbed my clothes and followed them down the hall and out into the sunlight. The days were getting longer. George got into a car with someone. The car was pulling away as Albert came out. He pointed at George and yelled, "I'll get you, motherfucker. I'll get you if I got to come to your house."

"Forget it," I said.

"I ain't gonna forget nothin," he said.

The others stood on the curb and lighted cigarettes. They were talking quietly.

"It doesn't mean anything," I said.

"He ain't gonna give me no bloody nose and get away with it," Albert ranted. He joined the group on the sidewalk. Someone handed him a cigarette. He lighted it and threw the match into the gutter. They crossed the parking lot in the biting air, splashing long shadows in the distant sun.

We used to fight, too. The battlefield was usually the school playground, a field bordered by oaks and elms beside a pond. There were ducks and swans on the pond. Beyond it was the Town Hall. As the fight developed, a delighted crowd would surround it. The fighters would drop their books on the grass. There was some preliminary pushing. Then they would close and clutch each other desperately. Grunting and wheezing, they dipped and swayed. Their faces would be very red. They would topple. The kid who landed on top was the winner. The kid on the bottom writhed and squirmed and swore until he got tired and ran out of words. Pretty soon the audience got bored and drifted away. The winner lay on top till the wriggling underneath subsided. He waited a bit to make sure. All he could feel was the rise and fall of weary breathing. He got up and went home to dinner. The loser would be too tired to try anything else. His shirt would be grass-stained. His top button would be torn off. If it wasn't too dark, he would look for it in the grass.

I stopped counting the fights in the gym that winter. There was an attack with a chair, an attack with a pop bottle. Every time I tore them apart, the punches zipped past my head and shoulders. But I never got more than a cut lip or bruised chin.

There was a nucleus of about ten ballplayers, who came nearly every Monday and Wednesday. I knew them only on the basketball court. Who you were depended on what you could do with a basketball. They expressed themselves with their wrists, their legs, and their style. I had to speak to them the same way. The only one who knew me better was George.

George finished school at one thirty. He used to come see us. Sometimes he joined my classes. Sometimes he helped Mrs. Brooks with her children. His father worked for Ford. George was one of five children. They lived on Leslie near the Lodge Expressway. Mr. Bucknell made decent money and the house was solid and tidy. George was seventeen, in the tenth grade at Central High. He was studying first year Spanish. His marks weren't good, but then he didn't work. He thought he would like to get a job with Ford when he got out of school. He loved to dance, get high on marijuana, and play basketball. He played basketball every time he could slip into an empty gym. He played in alleys and on asphalt playgrounds. He played before school and after school.

When George peeled off his shirt to play basketball, you could see a gray scar like a low-hanging watch chain across his stomach. It had happened that summer. George was walking along Glendale Avenue with Jeffrey and Albert Glass. It was after midnight. There was a man at the corner of Glendale and Woodrow Wilson. He darted out of the shadows and shoved a knife deep into George's belly. George collapsed as the man vanished. The Glass boys sprinted down Twelfth Street till they found a police car. George was taken to Metropolitan Hospital. He was on the critical list for three days. The man who stabbed him had mistaken him for someone else. What was the use of pressing charges?

Our friendship was a little hard on George. I depended on him. I made sure of his approval when a new kid showed up. If the kid was a bad one, I waited for George to tell him to get out. I tried to be on his team.

Once Jeffrey Glass was getting tough with George. I brushed George during a pause and whispered an appeal to him not to fight. He nodded. Jeffrey kept leaning and hacking. George concentrated on his game. He started shooting from twenty feet out and scoring. Jeffrey bumped him, and when he lunged George danced around him and scored from in close. Jeffrey got frantic. George turned his back on every challenge and tossed the ball into the basket. It was too much for Jeffrey. He threw a wild punch. George spun away, still not biting. I grabbed Jeffrey and backed him into a corner. His handsome face was contorted.

"I'm gonna kill him," he spat. "I don't care if he is your buddy, Mr. Hough. I'm gonna kill him."

My buddy. I had made an unfair demand on George. I should have let Jeffrey go. But I held tight.

Later I thanked George. He shrugged. I shouldn't have said anything.

One sticky afternoon the principal walked into the gym in the middle of a game. We stopped. The principal halted, alone on the gym floor. The kids looked at him as though he were a policeman without his uniform or gun. He smiled, diffident and embarrassed. He always worried that they were going to break windows or light fires. He couldn't understand that all they wanted to do was play basketball.

"Yes?" I said. I was oozing sweat and breathing hard. The kids were silent. They all stared at the principal.

"I need some help in the office," he said. "I need about four boys. It'll just take fifteen minutes."

The kids gaped. "Shee-it," someone whispered.

"Doing what?" I said.

"Folding and stapling some papers."

I needed time to think. "Let us finish this game," I said. "We'll be up in five minutes."

"Fine," he said. "Fine." He scurried out.

George regarded the door as it swung shut. "Let him do it hisself," he snapped.

A kid named Bobby said, "He can kiss my ass."

"Let's play ball," I said. We went back to the game and forgot about it. After the last point I grabbed the ball and stood under the basket.

"Look," I said. "I have to go up there. You don't have to. But it would be some favor to me if you did." No one moved. They studied the floor or stared at the sky through the high, wire-covered windows. I spotted George. He wouldn't look at me. They had got to him.

"Come on, Mr. Hough." It was the big kid named Bobby. He was pulling on his shirt. A year ago he had stolen three record players and a tape recorder from our audiovisual room. I loved him.

It was all right for George to come now. He scooped up his shirt without a word. Bennie, whom I had promised a summer job, was next. I had to turn down the fourth offer. We had enough.

We marched up to the office. The papers and staplers were laid out for us. It took fifteen minutes.

"Thanks," I said afterwards. More thanks than I could ever convey.

"Some day I'm gonna break his fuckin glasses," George said.

"You ain't lyin," Bobby said.

I thought I might get closer to them if we could play together as a team. And I was able to arrange a game with a men's club out in the suburbs. The captain of their team was named Gary. Fifteen years ago he had been an All-American at Princeton. He was an enormous, pink man in superb condition. He was very pleasant. He invited us to a school gym in his town.

George came to see me every day that week. We created intricate plays and argued about what defense we should use. He typed a roster, listing himself as captain and me as coach. We had to choose seven ballplayers. It was hard to eliminate the names of kids who had been playing with us all winter. But no one complained.

I met them in front of the school in the car owned by the Commission on Children and Youth. They were clustered on the steps in the dying light holding canvas satchels and smoking cigarettes. They rushed the car and tumbled in.

It was a half-hour drive. There were five in the back seat. I told them about Gary's team. It was a collection of former college stars. They were all older than thirty-five, but they were in shape. They had never lost. They had played the city high school champion and a group of Detroit Lions football players who played basketball in the off season. The kids listened while I talked. They didn't say much. They stared solemnly at the suburban twilight.

The school was new. The gym floor gleamed under the lights. The backboards were made of fiber glass. The locker room was dry and airy, with an antiseptic smell of powders and ointments that took me back to the locker room at Haverford. The boys examined everything. Gary greeted us warmly.

They were good. They were big and strong. They worked together as though they were computerized. They knew how to perforate a defense. They knew how to close lanes. At the end of the first half they led by ten points.

We sank to the floor and sprawled against the collapsible bleachers. We were dripping and gasping.

"Maybe they'll get tired," Bobby said.

"Maybe," I said.

The referee caught my eye. He wasn't the regular man, and he didn't know basketball. I picked myself up and scuffed over to him.

"I just want to tell you," he said, "your boys are unethical." He wore a silk undershirt and yellow pants. He had a woman's ass and he walked funny. I don't know where they ever found him.

"What do you mean?" I said.

"They're unethical. They're using their hands all kinds of ways. They're playing dirty."

"Playing dirty?" He should have come to our school sometime. The kids were on their best behavior tonight. No one on Gary's team had complained.

"Do you know where they come from?" I said. "Do you know what they're used to?" The kids were watching us, sitting in a line along the floor. I would have fought all the township for them.

"I know all about that," the ref said.

"Well then," I said.

"But they have to be taught," he said. "They have to learn."

"Fuck it," I said. "If you see a foul, call it."

"I will then," he said.

"You do that," I said.

He called more than ten fouls on us in the second half. Those people didn't miss the foul shots. They kept the pressure on us. We fought their size and practiced skill with hustle and instinctive finesse. We made them work. They beat us by twenty points.

After the game Gary's team surrounded us and shook our hands. They were hearty men with a stylized Ivy-league warmth. The kids received them graciously. We took showers and rubbed ourselves with fluffy white towels supplied by the school. We drifted out.

"You ought to be proud of them," Gary told me. He had been prepared for the worst. I thanked him.

It was a clear, warm night. The kids were exhilarated. It was a noisy drive home. They started in on the referee.

"Man, he got to be a fairy."

"You ever seen a cat walk like that?"

"God*damn*."

Later they sang, wailing a soulful edition of "This Guy's in Love with You." Albert Glass told a story about a friend of his who had tried selling tea and saying it was marijuana. They sang some more. We were home.

"Dig you later, Mr. Hough."

"You bet," I said.

They usually chose me when teams were picked. I was good enough, just barely. But my style was as different from theirs as the color of my skin. They were loose and unhampered, abandoned to the ecstasy of motion. They played ball the way they danced. I was too careful. I clanked up and down the court in a white suit of mail. I wanted to shed it and fly, but the more I thought, the stiffer I became. I started to miss shots. I was afraid to dribble. I was strangling myself.

A Peck of Salt

Our best ballplayers were Wiggie and Kenny. They could have made any college freshman team in the country. They were quiet boys. They avoided talking to me.

Kenny was powerful and chunky, but very quick. He would bring the ball down court, dribbling easily, his eyes roving. It was as though an invisible thread joined his hand to the ball, which rose and fell obediently. If someone swiped at the ball, it bounced between Kenny's legs and he picked it up behind his back with his other hand. Sometimes he would shoot from outside. Sometimes he would feint with his head and spring past his opponent and lay the ball in the basket. Or he might stare at the basket or into the face of his opponent and snap a pass to someone who had sneaked into the open. You would swear Kenny had never looked at the man, and suddenly that man had the ball.

Wiggie had a waist as thin as a little girl's. His strong arms and legs looked as though they had been chiseled out of copper. His front teeth jutted. His hands looked as though they could perform surgery, or carve a whalebone. Wiggie ran when he got the ball. He swept up and down the court like a leaf blown by an eddying wind, rollicking in endless motion. He could put the ball in the basket almost any time he wanted to.

Their skills bound Wiggie and Kenny together wordlessly. It didn't matter whether they were teammates. One complimented a good play by the other with a glance or nod.

128

A Peck of Salt

One day I had the job of guarding Wiggie. The first
time he got the ball he started to dribble, and I hovered
in front of him. He fluttered, like a character in an old
silent movie. I felt as though I were running under-
water. He darted one way, then another, and I lunged
back and forth like a careening truck. I was going one
way and he went the other and dropped the ball in the
basket.

He went to work on me. He spun right and left, he
bounded into open lanes, he dodged and faked and
sprinted. His shots bit the net. He was concentrating on
me. I caught glances and winks. They were watching
me. I felt a flash of panic. I slogged on, sweating plenti-
fully. I felt as though I had been undressed when the
game ended.

I walked off the floor, my eyes down. My throat was
tight. Wiggie and Kenny were talking. I heard my name.
They laughed. I trudged out into the hall and sat on the
window ledge until everyone had gone home.

I envied those kids. It was spring, and the sun was
new and warm on Twelfth Street. A swarm of boys was
playing dodgeball against the wall of the school. I wasn't
as free as I had thought I was.

We played until June. After that I saw them very seldom. Occasionally I passed Bobby or the Glass brothers
on Twelfth Street or Woodrow Wilson. George disappeared. Then one night in July he telephoned me.

"Hey," he said. "I'm back."

129

"Where you been?"

"I been stayin with my cousin in Monroe." Monroe was a town outside Detroit.

"You got a job yet?" I asked.

"Naw." He had been scouring the neighborhood for a job all spring. I realized that he had just called to say hello.

"Come on over to the school and see me," I said. "I'm teaching summer session."

"Okay."

"Good to have you back. You come on over. I want to see you."

"Okay," he said.

I never saw him again. Maybe he went back to Monroe. George was the only one of the basketball players who knew I was anything besides a bad dribbler with no left hand. He knew that too. He forgave me for it.

SIX

THE ASSISTANT PRINCIPAL stuck his head in the door
and waved me over. Dusty bars of sunlight filled the
hall. It was May.

"Did you hear about Taylor Smith?" the assistant
principal asked.

"No." He was the first boy who had come to me for
tutoring, the one with the amazing grin.

"His father came home last night abusing his mother
the way he does, and she stabbed him. Killed him."

"Killed him?"

"Yeah." He stood with his hands in his pockets and
gazed out the window, rocking slightly on the balls of
his feet. "Taylor won't be in school this week."

I had met Mrs. Smith. She was a good-looking
woman with narrow eyes and a very hard face. When
she had invited me in, she sat down with her chin in her
hands and listened to me talk about Taylor's school
work as though I were speaking a foreign language. She
had seven boys. They lived upstairs in a shabby house
on Davison near Twelfth Street. The flat wasn't as de-
cayed as some I had seen, but it was worn-out and
dreary.

The stabbing settled a long feud. Years ago Mr. and Mrs. Smith had decided that the only way they could live in the same house was without seeing each other. So the father took a job on the night shift at the Ford factory, the mother on the day shift in a hospital. Still, they kept colliding. Mr. Smith would come home drunk. They shouted abuse at each other. They spat and shoved. Once Mrs. Smith shot him in the leg with a .22 pistol. The police took him to the hospital and then left both of them alone. They knew all about Mr. and Mrs. Smith. Taylor and his brothers sometimes had to help their mother put down their father. Once he grabbed a meat cleaver. They surrounded him. Taylor knocked him down with a chair. I don't know how Taylor stayed as cheerful as he did.

Taylor came in later that morning. He was wearing dark glasses and his heavy black coat with the collar up around his neck. I could see his eyes through the lenses of the glasses. They were deepened and dilated by recent or imminent tears. His mouth was tight. He stared gravely through his vulnerable eyes. He moved deliberately. All this could have been changed then. It had not set, but the bitterness would harden fast.

There was a kid with him. He looked like Taylor at age twelve.

"Is there anything I can do?" I asked Taylor.

He shook his head. He hadn't come for anything special. He had just come.

I looked at the kid. "Your brother, right?"

Taylor nodded.

"What's your name?"

"Tasker."

"I'm Mr. Hough." We shook hands. "Your brother is one of my top men."

I pulled a pen and a scrap of paper out of my pocket and scribbled my telephone number. "If there's anything I can do, call me."

Taylor dropped the piece of paper into his big coat pocket. He was fifteen, and last night he had seen the blood of his father on the hands of his mother. Taylor had gone down and watched him die.

"You never know," I said. "There might be something I could do."

"My uncle say he gonna kill my mother," Taylor said. It was the first time he had spoken. His voice was husky and tired.

It was a fine May morning. At home people would be rigging their sailboats and heading out into Vineyard Sound.

"We got to slide on," Taylor said. "Got to go down to court."

"Your mother needs you," I said. "Take care of her."

"Yeah."

"I know you can take care of her," I said.

"Yeah, we can take care of her."

"Thanks for coming," I said. "You didn't have to come."

They nodded and walked away down the long hall, slowly and steadily with their hands in their pockets and their collars up.

That afternoon Taylor's brother Rick came in. This was just before Rick ran away from the boys' home and got busted for robbing the store.

"If I'd of been there, it wouldn't of happened," he told me. "Taylor was sleepin, see, and he didn't wake up soon enough. They was fightin all over the place. Chairs and tables knocked over, busted the TV set." He talked fast and used his hands. "Taylor woke up, but he was in a daze, you know what I mean? He heard the noise, but he was in a daze and didn't know what was happenin. By the time he got out there, she had the knife up in his belly. Now me, I wake up fast, you know?"

Taylor started to change. He came to school less. He had things going in the neighborhood. His mother and brothers moved to another house with relatives, and Taylor went away by himself and got an apartment with friends. He was dealing in drugs. He sold marijuana and barbiturates, and later I heard he was getting into heavier stuff. The kids at school knew they could get it from him. He started wearing new clothes. He was doing all right.

"What if you get caught?" I said.

Taylor shrugged. His old smile was coming back. "It's like everything else," he said. "If you don't try nothin, you don't get nothin." He leaned across the table. "You gonna tell me it's wrong, ain't you, Mr. Hough?" I started to say something. "But I got more now than I ever had. You want me to go work out at Ford like my father? Where did my father get workin at Ford?"

"What do you want to do later?" I said.

"I want to travel," he said.

"Where to?"

"All over, man. All over the world."

"Where you going to get the money?" I asked.

"Don't worry about me," he said. "I can get along, you know what I mean?"

I had never heard a ghetto kid say he wanted to travel. Taylor didn't know that travel was for white kids with rich grandmothers. I saw a black man in Venice one time. He was strolling in the Piazza San Marco. It was a warm August morning. The square glittered like a picture by Canaletto. The black man wore a plaid shirt and carried a camera on a strap around his neck. He was walking slowly and gazing up at the great spires of the Church of Saint Mark. A little Italian who must have been hustling something crept up behind him. "Hey, baby." He sang it like a child teasing a younger brother about a speech defect, bending forward, thrusting his head like a bird. The black man turned and looked steadily at the swarthy runt. He was tall and straight and the Italian looked like a crooked dwarf beside him. He smiled softly, and the thing I noticed was that he wasn't surprised. He turned his back on the Italian and went on studying the façade of the cathedral.

"If you really want to do something, you can do it," Taylor said.

I wanted to tell him about the black man in Venice. I wanted to warn him. But all I said was, "Just don't get caught dealing dope."

"Don't worry." He smiled his big smile. "I'm cool."

One night I got a glimpse of the people who had scored the way Taylor Smith wanted to. I was drinking beer by myself at the Trade Winds, the bar that the librarian had taken Beth and me to that night we went out. I was getting to know Bill, the singer. I bought him a drink. He ordered a vodka gimlet and swallowed it with one gulp.

"Come and eat with me after we close," he said.

Bill finished his last set at two. He put his guitar in its case and led me out the door to his Thunderbird. He flicked on the radio and sped along Seven Mile Road to the Lodge Expressway, then to Livernois Avenue. On Livernois he nosed the Thunderbird into a jammed parking lot beside a garish restaurant.

"This is where the hustlers come after the bars close," Bill said.

It was a long room, brightly lighted. The walls were wide varnished planks. The lights were models of old street lamps. It was nice, but the lights and noise made it seem cheap. Every booth was stuffed, every table surrounded. The customers were black. Most of the men had women. The men were all ages, but their women were all young and good-looking. Some had white women. All wore splendid clothes.

Bill and I stood near the door beside the jukebox and waited for a table. A woman on her way out with her man stopped and stared at Bill. "I know you," she said. She was all Afro, her hair a huge bulb, big gold earrings, a coat like leopard skin. "You used to sing over at the Townsman."

"That's right," Bill said.

The proprietors were white men. They kept sharp eyes on everything. They had sagging bellies and skin that looked like dough. Against the hard, vigorous black men, they looked as though they had been living for years under stones. One of them led us to a booth.

While we studied the menu, a tall, well-built man sauntered past. "Reggie," Bill said. Reggie was light-skinned, his hair processed and carefully clipped. "Reggie, this is my friend John." I stood up and shook hands with Reggie. He was wearing a tan jacket and matching turtleneck sweater. He gave Bill a clap on the shoulder and moved on.

"Did you notice the ring he was wearing?" Bill said.

"Yeah."

"He paid five thousand in cash for it."

"What does he do?" I asked.

Bill leaned forward and spoke quietly. "He's a numbers man. Works for his father. Thousands of dollars go through his hands every week. Man, you ought to see his house."

The waitress stood over us, holding her pad and pencil up under her nose. She was a pretty soul sister. She smiled out of the corner of her lipsticked mouth.

"What you got good?" Bill said.

"They ain't nothin bad, brother," she said.

"We could dig steak and eggs," Bill said.

She snatched the menus and headed for the kitchen.

A blue-black giant with a goatee stopped in front of us. "What's happenin?" he said. He was wearing a long coat with a mink collar. Bill reached up and shook his hand.

"Roy, this is John," Bill said. I got halfway up and shook Roy's hand.

"Pleased to meet you," Roy said. He leaned down and whispered something into Bill's ear. Bill whispered back, and they laughed and slapped palms.

"Dig you later," Roy said.

"There goes one of the biggest pimps on the West Side," Bill said.

The waitress came back with our steaks and eggs. They were served on oval wooden plates with stacks of yellow-brown toast. The steak was rare, and the egg yolks split and flowed into the red juice. Reggie came back and slid in beside Bill. He had been sitting several booths away with two girls.

"No action," he said. The girls paid and walked past us, switching their tails and smirking at Reggie.

"You sure?" Reggie said.

They giggled and shook their heads.

"Damn," Reggie said. He had a nasal, musical voice.

"Ain't that chick married?" Bill said.

"Yeah," Reggie said. "Seems to be some kind of trouble, though. She in here every night."

An older woman passed with two young queens at her heels. Reggie examined them. "Excuse me," he said to the last in line. "Is that lady your mother?"

The girl nodded.

"Out with Mama, huh?"

The girl nodded. The others were walking on.

"Ain't that nice," Reggie said. "That's very nice." She started off. "Hey." She paused, looking back over her shoulder. "Would it be possible for me to meet your sister?"

The girl smiled. She had nice, even teeth. "You'd have to talk to her about that." She was gone.

"Shee-it," Reggie whistled. Bill winked at me.

As we were getting up, a man chewing a toothpick tapped Bill on the shoulder. "Listen, man," he said. "I got to talk to you." He was opening a nightclub, and the first night was going to be a special show. He needed a master of ceremonies.

"No, man, I'm too busy," Bill said. "Maybe Reggie can help you."

" 'Fraid not, man," Reggie drawled.

A young man in a gray jacket with brass buttons, gray pants, and buckled shoes walked in. Bill waved him over. He was a disk jockey. He liked the sound of the job. He and the nightclub owner set up an appointment, and the big man waddled out.

The disk jockey tossed a light left jab against Reggie's shoulder. "You givin a party tonight, Reggie?"

"Maybe. Who you bringin?"

The kid laughed. He had the compact build of a fighter. "Later, man," he said, and sat down at a booth filled with men and women his age.

"Nice meetin you," Reggie said, and shook my hand again.

Bill and I pushed through the swinging glass door into the chilly morning. It was almost four. The parking lot was still full, but there were no cars out on Livernois.

"Most of the cats in there have some kind of hustle goin," Bill told me as we slid into the Thunderbird.

"What about you?" I said.

"I got my singin." He nosed the car onto Livernois, and it sprinted like a cat in first and second gears.

"But if you didn't have your singing," I said, "would you have a hustle then?"

He patted the dashboard. "If I wanted to drive this, I would."

Taylor Smith was going to hustle his way out of baggy overalls and the tenements along Davison. If it worked, it would be quick. There were other, slower roads. They were long and circuitous and finally ended close to where they had begun. They were the roads that white society approved of. They started in the ghetto and ended three or four blocks away, in the wealthy black sections of Chicago and Boston Boulevards, and on streets like Edison and Fullerton. Here, tucked beside the wasteland of Twelfth Street, lived pockets of black people who had made some of the white man's money.

I went to a party at one of those houses the night before Erlinda Ngayan left Detroit. She was going home to Los Angeles to take some education courses. The party was in the basement of a young married couple on Edison, two houses away from the people who had housed Erlinda all year. Mike and Rene were their relatives. It was a gathering of the clan. They had all come to say good-bye to Erlinda. Almost all were married, almost all middle-aged. I was the only white person. For the first time I felt the difference in Erlinda's and my races. She circulated, dark Philippine eyes and caramel skin, among the black people who had come to accept her as part of their family.

There were kisses on the cheek and warm handshakes as the guests came in. The men wore sweaters and sportshirts. The women wore dresses from the seventh floor of Hudson's Department Store.

Mike was an architect, with a master's degree from the University of Pennsylvania. He was tall and angular, with a crew cut. He wore a white shirt open at the neck and rolled up at the wrists. The guests tumbled down the cellar stairs and Mike scooted around behind the bar and started making drinks. He poured the liquor from high off the counter and cracked jokes. He looked like a Princeton boy.

Rene had grown up near Philadelphia and Mike had found her while he was at Penn. She was short and nicely built and had a face that you knew had seen plenty.

Red and blue lights beamed on the paneled walls. There was a picture of Martin Luther King, some Expressionist prints, and a blown-up color photograph of a Vermont landscape. Records by Jose Feliciano, Otis Redding, and Dionne Warwick were fed onto the stereo. A table was spread with potato salad, cold ham, and hors d'oeuvres that looked as though they had come out of tiny, expensive cans. Mike poured the drinks fast and strong, and by ten everyone was high.

They began getting up off the chairs and barstools to dance. They did a sedate ballroom dance that evolved, as the drinks kept coming, into an awkward imitation of the dancing my kids did. The men took turns dancing with Erlinda. She smiled like a Southern belle and accepted each as though it were her special pleasure. I stayed on a barstool and sipped my bourbon.

Then Gloria Wattles, who worked for the Commission on Children and Youth, got up to dance with her husband; a long black reed of a man. When I was introduced to him, he had measured me with the keen, unflinching stare of the black militant. He had natural hair and a goatee. He got up slowly and danced with a well-timed but lethargic fluidity, as though he were saving his energy for more important things.

Almost everyone was dancing. I sat at the bar with my bourbon and listened to the music. I felt as though I were on a boat, drifting away across the water from these people. I began to think about Ellie.

"There's a soul sister in the office at Peck that wants to go out with you," the librarian had told me a week ago.

"What?"

"She was a secretary in our office for a while." Peck was a mile from our school, between Woodrow Wilson and Twelfth Street. "I got the word from a secretary over there. Her name's Ellie."

I remembered Ellie. She was tall and lovely.

"She wants to go out with me?"

"Here's your chance to broaden your Vista experience."

Flatter us, and we will do anything. I called Ellie and asked her to lunch. The thought of going out with a soul sister was like the prospect of making love for the first time. It was the idea, the promise, that was exciting. Late one afternoon I had been walking along Woodward Avenue, close to the center of the city. The Broderick Tower and Hudson's shot up into the dusk in front of me, tiers and tiers of tiny lights. The bars and burlesque halls along Woodward were getting noisy. The hustlers were out.

"You look like you lookin for a good time." It was a black man in a purple suit. "I got both kinds, white and black. You can take your pick, sir."

"No thanks," I said.

White and black. The phrase ran in and out of me. I walked on in the dusk amid the red and white city lights. Fantastic images of black women slithered in the shadows.

Larry donated his car to the project. I met Ellie in the office of the Peck School at noon. She was sitting behind a typewriter. Her green dress hung elegantly on her sinuous frame. I held her coat for her. Two young black teachers watched me.

I opened the car door for Ellie and we scooted down the ramp onto the expressway. I sheered into the passing lane and the librarian's sports car outran everyone to our right.

"Where are you from?" Ellie asked.

"Massachusetts."

"Massachusetts?" She said it as though I had just told her I was married. "Massachusetts?"

"What's wrong with Massachusetts?"

"You have a funny accent. I never heard an accent like yours. I thought you might be English."

"English?" *English?* Christ.

She bit her lower lip. It was red-orange against her smooth brown skin.

I slowed too suddenly and a car almost skidded into

our stern. The driver belted his horn. I crept into the center lane and up the ramp to Grand Boulevard.

"Are you nervous?" she blurted.

"No," I muttered.

The restaurant was clean and varnished and full of white people who must have worked in the Fisher Building. Ellie put her elbows on the table and asked me about my work. I described the job.

"I bet they give you a rough time," she said.

"Some of them do."

"I can't see it," she said. "Why do you do it?" We were sitting beside a window. I watched the people stream past.

"I don't know why I do it," I said. "To stay out of the army. To learn."

"What kind of background do you come from?" she asked.

I told her about Cape Cod and Haverford College.

"I thought so," she said. "Have you ever been out with a colored girl before?"

"No." I was beginning to feel as though I were being hunted. But I thought I could satisfy her with my answers.

"I didn't think you'd been out with a colored girl. You were nervous driving over here, weren't you?"

"I suppose so," I said.

"Why did you ask me out?"

I dropped my head and chuckled into the bright silverware. "Why do you think?" The waitress came and set down our plates. "Why did you accept?"

Ellie shrugged and picked up her fork. "My mother told me not to." She started eating, very neat and dainty. "You seemed pretty real," she said. "You seemed sincere. I thought it would be nice to talk to you." She stared out the window. "Besides. Going out to lunch with someone is nothing. You can go out to lunch with anyone." Her gaze came back from the busy sidewalk. "But I'll tell you," she said softly, "I'm prejudiced."

"I'm not," I said.

Her eyes narrowed. "Everyone is," she snapped.

"I don't know about that," I said.

"Listen," she said. "One of the reasons I decided to go out with you was because I thought you were English. Foreigners are less prejudiced than Americans."

"All right," I said. "If you look at someone and decide to like him because of what's inside him, are you prejudiced?"

"I'll say you're fair," she said. "I'll give you that, but that's all."

"Being fair is the same as not being prejudiced," I said.

She smiled. "Everyone's prejudiced," she said. "I grew up in poverty. I know what it's like to be poor and black. I know what white folks can do."

"Would you believe me if I said I was truly sorry?" I

said. I stared into my empty coffee cup. "Would you believe me if I said I truly hate what my people have done to your people?"

"But you can't feel it like I can." Her brown eyes burned. "I hate what white people have done to Indians. But it doesn't make me boil up. Not like I do when I think about what's been done to my people."

She was right. I could never boil the way she could. I glanced at my watch. The girl brought the check and I dropped some bills onto the little tray.

In front of the Peck School I reached across Ellie's lap and opened the door for her. "Thank you," she said. "I enjoyed lunch."

"Maybe I'll see you around," I said.

"Maybe," she said. I watched her walk away. You could picture her under that coat. I shoved the car into first gear and drove slowly back to school, crawling home wounded.

Mike's wife Rene was still behind the bar. Everyone else was reeling on the dance floor. Rene spotted me alone and came over to talk. She was clutching a drink. She was as high as any of them. She leaned on the counter like a bartender. She asked me where I'd gone to school. I told her Haverford, and she slapped her broad thigh. She had grown up in Bryn Mawr.

Rene used to skate on the campus pond. I asked where her home was, and she tried to explain. It was almost adjacent to the campus, but I had never seen it. It was in a pocket of poor black people. I had lived four years on a campus with oaks and cherry trees and lovely old stone buildings and never known those black people were there.

"I don't know how I missed them," I said.

Rene laughed. It was an ironic laugh, spiced with contempt. "Your people have been missing it right along," she said. "Nothing to be surprised about."

I stared into my drink, at the ice floating in the yellow whiskey.

Rene told me about her childhood. She had no father. There were six children. They were hungry. Her brothers were fine athletes. They had broken track records at Haverford High School, and two of them had had athletic scholarships at Villanova.

Willie Thomas, our supervisor from the Commission on Children and Youth, walked in. He had been at another party. Rene poured him a drink and he sat down beside me. The dancers were getting tired. Gloria came over for another drink. Rene talked on, leaning on the bar and sipping hers. Willie was following our conversation very carefully. Rene told of the cruelties of white people to her and her family in Bryn Mawr. The bourbon made me feel far away. I watched Gloria's husband, like an African king in a ruffled white shirt, dancing with Erlinda. For an instant I hated my white high school, my Beethoven symphonies, my trips to Europe.

"Look," I said. "I'm sorry. I'm truly sorry."

Willie smiled.

"What can I do?" I said.

Rene sipped her drink. Willie said nothing. "I don't know," Rene said. "Just to know what's happening is something."

"I think I know what's happening," I said.

"You think you do," Rene said.

"All right," I said. "Maybe I don't know anything. What can I do?"

"You're doing something in Vista," Rene said.

Gloria was sitting on the other side of Willie. "Vista volunteers," she said. "What's a Vista volunteer? A Vista volunteer ain't nothin." If a white person had told me that, I would have told him to shove it. Now I only stared into my glass of bourbon. The ice was melting and the bourbon was getting pale.

"But Gloria," I said. I felt surrounded. "In a few cases I'm doing some good. You can help a few individual kids, don't you think?"

She said nothing. Rene put her hand on my arm. "Don't worry, honey," she said. "Don't worry."

Sure. Don't worry. When justice rules at last, you too will burn. You will perish with the corrupt legislators and judges, the corporation presidents and chiefs of police. Cape Cod and the Elizabeth Islands will be scoured and blackened by the fire that will cleanse you and your race.

I finished my drink. I felt tired and far away. The party was breaking up. I trudged up the cellar steps and out into the May evening. You could smell the new leaves and lawns along Edison. It seemed impossible that Twelfth Street was one block away. The guests were saying good-bye to Rene and Mike at the front door. There was laughter. Gloria's husband glided out, tall and lean with that easy grace that seemed to promise so much more movement sometime soon.

Willie Thomas drove me home. The streetlights glowed feebly on scraps of newspaper and bits of glass on Twelfth Street. A few drops of rain hit the windshield. Once when I was very small I was in a rowboat with a man from New York, a friend of the family who had come to our summer cottage for a weekend. He had asked me if I wanted to go rowing with him. It turned out he didn't know how to row. We were dragged away by the current. The man didn't notice the current until he tried to row back. He pointed toward home and yanked and thrashed with the oars, and we inched backwards. I was sitting in the stern. I could see the dock in the distance. The sun was going down behind our house. The man chopped the water with the oars. We were tugged backwards. I started to cry.

"We're going to miss Erlinda," Willie said.

III

He Can't Stand to Care

SEVEN

ROBERT SIMMONS and I had begun our odyssey in September, several weeks before he had told me, "When you think you can get away with something you got to try."

I remember how he filled the library doorway that first day.

"Are you Mr. Hough?"

"That's right," I said. I was sitting in the late summer sunlight with Taylor and Tut. We were studying the Civil War.

"Mr. Gordon sent me up to see you."

"Good," I said. "What's your name?"

"Simmons. Robert." He frowned at Taylor and Tut and sat down. "Can I smoke?" he said.

"In here?" I said. "You want to smoke in the library?"

"Yeah, I want to smoke in the library."

"No," I said. "My God. I'd lose my job."

"He's right, man," Taylor said.

Robert glanced at him with slitted eyes. "Shut up, punk." Taylor inspected a page of his history book.

We went on with the lesson. Taylor and Tut took

turns reading, and I questioned them. Robert sat with his elbows on his knees and his head in his hands. He had a long, brooding face. It looked like a charred axe-head. He was wearing green slacks and a cashmere sweater with a low neck that showed a chest of polished bronze. He stared past us out the window at the blue September sky, looking bored and disgusted. The bell rang. Taylor and Tut sauntered out into the traffic in the hall. Robert sat there with his head in his hands.

"Who's supposed to be your teacher this hour?" I asked.

"Mrs. Richards." His jaw moved in his hand.

"Let's go see her," I said. "We'll tell her you're going to be with me."

We got up. I walked slowly and turned a couple of times so he could catch up to me, but he preferred to walk behind me. He was a foot taller than most of the kids we passed. He looked about nineteen.

I pushed open Mrs. Richards's door. She was a big boned, light brown woman.

"I'd like to work with Robert this hour, if it's all right with you," I said.

She stared at Robert. "Robert who?"

"This Robert. Robert Simmons."

"I don't know him."

"He's in your class," I said.

"He's not in my class."

Robert looked her over, his head tilted truculently. "I

am in your class." He had a husky voice, as though his throat were tight.

"You may be on the list, but you haven't been here yet," she said. Robert squinted at her.

"Well," I said busily, "will it be all right if I take him?"

"You can have him." She spun into her room and closed the door.

Robert blinked at the door. "Fuck you, lady," he purred.

The halls were empty now. "Okay," I said. "I'll see you tomorrow." He nodded and disappeared down the stairs.

Robert was fifteen, but he was much too old for junior high school. I don't know how long it had been since he had gone to classes regularly, but it was clear to me that he never would again. He had grown up too fast. He thought too much. Robert was impatient with the banalities of an eighth grade classroom. He would get furious at his own ignorance of fundamentals he could have learned half-asleep five years ago. I separated him from my other students and the principal gave me permission to mark him. I was the only teacher Robert had.

The first time we read I pushed aside the books I had been using with the other kids and opened my own copy of a paperback anthology of poems. I found some excerpts from "Song of Myself" and slid the book across the table. Robert stared at it as though it were a plate of cold beans.

"How about reading this?" I said.

He took a deep breath and reached up and pinned the book to the table. "Can I read it to myself?"

"I . . . . sure."

He shifted his weight and inserted his head like a hatchet into the book. His eyes contracted and he sucked in his cheeks.

I celebrate myself, and I sing myself,
And what I assume you shall assume,
For every atom belonging to me as good belongs to you.

His eyes inched across the page. He reread the verse. Five minutes passed. He let out a sigh and lifted his head and stared over my shoulder toward the Sears Building.

"Okay?" I said.

He nodded.

"Do you have any idea what this is about?" I said.

His head sank almost to his chest. He studied his lap. "I guess this man sayin we all in it together."

I stared at him. Yes, yes. "Tremendous," I said. I leaned forward and flipped questions at him. He answered hesitantly, doubtfully, deep in his throat. He had understood what he had read. He could calculate it in his own terms.

I finished. Robert studied his lap. I slapped the table.

"You know how good this is?" I said. Two girls at the next table were watching. They looked puzzled.

Robert gazed into his lap.

"It's good enough for a senior in high school, that's how good it is," I said.

He lifted his head just enough to see me. He smiled for a moment. "You jivin me," he said, and smiled again.

He came to school two or three times a week. We read Langston Hughes and Countee Cullen, then started *The Old Man and the Sea.* We worked about an hour a day and he did some reading at home.

One morning he closed his book before we had finished. "Hey," he said. "My mother talkin trash about me not bein in school. She thinks I don't never come, because I didn't used to be goin."

"Would you like me to talk to her?"

"Yeah."

It was a golden autumn morning. We crossed Twelfth Street and cut over to Woodrow Wilson. Robert led me to a little grocery store. Beside its smoky plate-glass window was a door. A sheet of plywood was nailed over it. Its handle was the loop of a twisted coathanger. We walked into a dark and narrow staircase, a murk reeking of beer and urine. The steps squeaked. Another plywood slab held together the door to the Simmons flat. Robert rapped and pushed it open. We walked down the dilapidated hall to the living room. Wholesome sunlight bored through the window that looked down on Woodrow Wilson. There was an old gray sofa and a television on a table in the corner. The wallpaper hung like luffing sails. Mrs. Simmons sat like a bag of shot dropped on the sofa.

Her eyes seemed huge. "Pleased to meet you," she said. I shook her hand. "Sit down," she said. I sat on the edge of a ragged armchair. Robert sat on the arm of the sofa, his elbows on his knees, his eyes on the floor.

"Robert's told me all about you," Mrs. Simmons said.

"I just came to let you know he's been coming to school."

"That's good," she said. "It's the first time, I'm tellin you."

"See?" Robert barked. "You don't never listen to me."

"You hush," she snapped over her shoulder.

"And he's doing some amazing work," I said.

"It sure is good to hear it," she said. "You drop in any time you want to. I'm mighty pleased to meet you."

"Nice to meet you."

She trailed me down the hall, scuffing in slippers. She was smiling as she shut the door behind me. I clattered down the steps and out into the glare on Woodrow Wilson.

The principal told me a story about the Simmons family. Mr. Simmons had gone away several years ago. But the boys still saw him around the neighborhood and they were friends. Robert especially was fond of his father. One afternoon while Mrs. Simmons was out, their father pulled up in front of the flat in a pickup truck. Robert and his brother were home. Their father told them that he and Mrs. Simmons had just decided to start together again in a new apartment a few miles away. He had come for the furniture. Robert and his brother helped Mr. Simmons load the furniture onto the truck, and the old man drove away. They never saw him again. When Mrs. Simmons came home, all that was left were the television, the sofa, and an old double bed. Robert told the guidance counselor that he was going to kill his father next time he saw him.

Robert stopped coming to school in October. I waited for him, leaning on the shelf at the window and watching the kids play touch football on the cindery playground below. It was still warm. Some of them took off their shirts to play. The sky was blue, with big, solid-looking clouds. I wondered why it was so lucid during the day, when at night you couldn't see the stars. I looked for Robert every time the library door opened.

I didn't go to his home. He wouldn't be there. And I didn't want anyone to force him to come to school. I figured he'd come back himself.

Report cards were handed out at the end of October. Robert must have heard about it from his brother. He came back to school. He sauntered in as though he'd never been gone. He was wearing the green slacks and a

new white sweater. The heels of his black shoes looked
as though they had been filed off.

"Look who's here," I said.

The librarian had tacked a menagerie of cardboard
animals along one wall, pink and yellow tigers and ele-
phants and alligators with idiot grins. Robert stopped
just inside the door and studied them.

"I think I remember you from somewhere," I said.

He couldn't help smiling. "Let's do some work," he
said.

"Guess what," I said. "Report cards come out today.
Isn't that a coincidence?"

The smile grew a little. He sat down. He stared into
his lap and the smile held on.

"You can get yours after school," I said.

Robert had spent about ten days in school. Every
time the guidance counselor asked about him I said he
was doing fine. I was sure he *was* going to do fine. But I
gave him three marks of D, which was just above failure.

After the last bell had rung Robert walked into the
library holding his report card as though it were a parking ticket.

"What's this?"

"What?" I was checking some spelling papers. There
was no one else in the library.

"You gave me D's, man."

"I know it."

"I don't deserve no D's."

"You deserve F's," I said. "I've only seen you about ten times."

He paced up and down in front of the table. He had a rolling walk, like a sailor's. "You gave Taylor and Tut C's."

"I know."

"That ain't right, Mr. Hough."

"They come to school."

"They don't read nothin like I been readin." He stopped and our eyes met. "Do they? Do they read stuff as hard as I been readin?"

"Of course not."

"All right, then." He stabbed the air with a downward thrust of his index finger.

"How can I give you good marks when I never see you?"

"But I'm better than Taylor and Tut. You said I was doin the best work. Now you sayin I ain't."

"Come on," I said. "I'll walk home with you."

Just then Taylor charged in. "I left my book in here," he panted.

Robert glared at him.

"What's happenin, Robert?" Taylor said. He had his report card.

"Shut your fuckin mouth," Robert growled. Taylor ducked out. "Punk," Robert murmured.

"Come on," I said. I pulled on my jacket. It had been raining. Twelfth Street was stained and slick, and the wind came from the west and shook the brown leaves of the trees along Buena Vista Avenue. Robert kept his eyes on the sidewalk.

"Listen," I said. "Say you're a teacher. You got a smart kid and a dumb one. The dumb one works and the smart one doesn't do anything. It isn't fair to the dumb one to give the smart one a better mark. The dumb one's been doing all the work."

We crossed Woodrow Wilson and stopped in front of the plywood-plastered door. Robert paused with his hand on the bent coathanger handle, as though he were waiting for me to finish a story.

"You don't think I'm stupid, do you, Robert?"

He shook his head.

"All right," I said. "I know brains when I see them, and you have them. There's nothing you can't do if you want to."

He glanced at me and then studied my face hungrily. Then his huge, convex eyelids dropped abruptly. He pushed open the door. The coathanger rattled as the door clamped shut.

He came back to school. We finished *The Old Man and the Sea* and read some of *The Autobiography of Malcolm X*. We started to talk. We spent many of our hours on the window ledge in the hall. It was a broad shelf, and we would perch there with our backs against the high panes, the light slanting down over our shoulders. After the first fifteen minutes Robert usually hopped down and leaned forward, his elbows planted on the ledge. Or he would pace, rubbing his big flat palms.

One day he led me nervously into the hall. "I think Sharon's pregnant," he said.

Sharon was a freshman at Central, a light-skinned girl with a pretty figure. She had a tranquil but knowing smile, like a Lippi Madonna who had just spent a weekend in Cannes with Richard Burton. Sometimes she came to school with Robert. She would sit beside him and wait. He talked tough to her. She listened, smiling her soft, ironic smile, and never interrupted our lessons.

"She might be sayin this to trap me," Robert said.

"Let's wait and make sure," I said. "No one's going to trap you yet."

Sharon was pregnant, all right. Her mother hadn't ever liked Robert. Now she hated him. She wouldn't let him in her house. Robert said she wanted to charge him with statutory rape. She came to school one time: a handsome, copper woman. She told me Robert was a vicious hoodlum. But she couldn't lock Sharon in, and Robert kept seeing her.

Another time Robert led me out urgently and said, "Can I ask you a favor?"

"Sure."

"Naw, you'll just get mad."

"Why should I get mad?"

"Naw, you gonna get mad."

"Look, just ask me."

"You think you can lend me two dollars?" He stared out the window, biting his lower lip.

His clothes were at the cleaner's. He couldn't reclaim them. He was wearing very dirty pants and an old sweater. He looked down at them as though they were prison clothes. Robert liked cashmere sweaters and bright slacks. On days that he was well dressed the roll in his gait was more pronounced and his head was a little higher. To me, blue meant Vineyard Sound on a breathless June morning. But Robert had never seen the ocean. The only real blue he knew was in the sweaters he saw in store windows, the slacks and the shoes that matched. I knew Robert's wardrobe. It was a small one. Now and then he swaggered in with a sweater or coat that I had never seen and never saw again.

"Sure," I said. "I can lend you two dollars."

He accepted it with a nod, not looking at me, and slid the bills slowly into his pocket. He asked to borrow money for the cleaner about a dozen times that year. Sometimes he paid me back.

Robert's friends often came to wait for him. They were older than Robert. They moved very carefully and kept their hands in their pockets. I was supposed to throw them out of the building. That would have been a laugh.

Robert ignored most of the kids in school. They all knew him, though. One lunch hour they egged him into an arm-wrestling match with my student, Walter. About twenty of us were sitting around gabbing in the library when the subject of relative strengths arose. Walter was huge. They called him "Hoss." Pitting him and Robert would settle some disagreements. They started hollering for the match. Robert smiled, eyes lowered. Walter shrugged. Robert pulled his sleeve back over his lean black arm, opened and closed his hand a couple of times, and they locked arms. The kids pressed around the table. Some of them made bets. Sharon was there. She sat silent and smiling, a slightly sinful Madonna. Robert's mouth tightened. Muscle ridged his forearm like a blue steel band. Their clasped hands shuddered. Walter's arm sagged. It sank imperceptibly, like the hand of a clock. The kids yelled like the crowd at a cockfight. In a final spasm Walter's arm plunged to the table. Robert smiled faintly and massaged the knuckles of his right hand. He glanced at Sharon.

"Who else wants to go?"

Taylor was next. Robert drove his hand down like a machine. Several others had to try. Some used two hands. Robert licked all of them.

Then someone yelled that I should challenge Robert. A dozen voices echoed him. They grabbed my shoulders and tried to shove me into the chair opposite Robert. Robert calmly kneaded his upper arm. I laughed and shook my head. They tugged on my arms. The bell rang. It was time to go and they scattered, leaving Sharon and Robert and me alone in the library. Robert unrolled his sleeve and flexed his arm. I think I could have beaten him.

One day Robert came to school with a small bulge under his coat. He kept patting it, like a child with a frog in his pocket.

"What's that?" I said.

"What?"

"You know what. What's under your coat, that's what."

We were in the library. Robert glanced around. He lifted the hem of his long black coat. There was a revolver stuck into his belt above his left thigh.

"Jesus Christ."

He dropped his coat. Sharon was with him. She had stopped going to school and came with Robert almost every day now.

"You know what will happen if you get caught with that?" I said.

"I'm hip."

"What are you going to do with it?" I said.

"I'm gonna get someone."

"Who?"

"See that dude over there?" Robert leaned forward so that his chin almost rested on the tabletop. He was squinting across the library at a kid named Milo. Milo lived in the halfway house on Burlingame. He was thin-lipped and morose and burly.

"What did he do?" I said.

"He been talkin' some shit to Sharon."

Milo was busy. He didn't seem to notice Robert. He

would peer into an open book, write something in a notebook, and peer back into the book.

"What did he say?"

Robert shifted his weight and leaned closer to me. He was wearing a hat with the brim bent down over his eyes. "Yesterday Sharon said she was goin' to the store to get some pickles. And he says, 'She better get some pickles because she ain't gonna get my pickle.' "

I couldn't help smiling. "So you're going to shoot him."

Robert glowered at Milo. Milo was absorbed in his work. They were the two biggest kids in the school and they both had reputations. Milo had run with a gang on the East Side.

"You better stay away from him," I said.

"You think I'm scared?" Robert put his hands on the table and shifted his weight to his feet. "I'll go fight him right now."

"He knows karate," I said.

"He what?" Robert settled back into his chair. Karate is a magic word in the ghetto. Knowing karate in the inner city is like being rich in the suburbs.

"He knows karate," I said. I was making it up.

"How do you know?"

"I just know."

"I don't care if he do know karate," Robert said, but he studied Milo carefully.

I persuaded Robert to do some work. We were reading Wilfred Owen and Robert liked the stark language. We talked about it. His eye kept roaming across the room to Milo.

Milo got up when the bell rang and stacked his books. Robert glowered at him as he lumbered out. Milo acted as though Robert were not there. This infuriated Robert. I admired the tactic.

"I think it would be a good idea to leave that gun home," I said.

Robert wasn't going to get a chance at Milo. Every day as soon as school ended a supervisor from the halfway house met Milo and Leon Stewart at the door and drove them home. Milo lived more than two miles from Robert and he was watched closely. They never met by chance on the street. I guess they didn't want each other enough to meet halfway between Woodrow Wilson and Burlingame. It was probably lucky for both of them.

On a Friday in midwinter I asked Robert if he would like to go with me to the Zefirelli movie of *Romeo and Juliet*.

"Where's it at?" Robert asked. We were in the hall, framed by the sunlight through our window.

"The Studio Eight Theater," I said. "Out on Greenfield."

"What kind of neighborhood?" Robert asked. "Colored or white?"

The Studio Eight Theater was far from the tenement

buildings and the broken glass. "Well, there'll be mostly white out there," I said.

Robert lifted his head and stared into the shadows at the end of the hall. "I don't want to go," he said.

"Why not?"

"I'm scared."

It was like hearing a heavyweight champion admit he's afraid of mice. A white suburb has no sharp edges, no abrasive extensions. Everything is wrapped in cotton.

"Nothing to it," I said.

He stood with his hands in his pockets and stared down the hall.

"All right?" I said.

He didn't answer.

"All right?"

He shrugged.

I told him I would pick him up at eleven thirty.

Next morning at eleven fifteen my phone rang. It was Robert. "Mr. Hough. I don't know if I can go."

"You have to go."

"I ain't got nothin to wear. My clothes are in the cleaner's. I ain't got enough money to get them out."

"Wear something dirty."

"I can't do that. All I need is fifty cents."

"I could lend you that," I said. "But we don't have time. I'll bring you a sweater."

"Damn," he said.

"I'll see you in a few minutes and I'll have a sweater for you."

"Damn."

I hung up.

It was like a spring day. The city seemed to glitter. I went out with no coat. I brought a sweater for Robert and drove the Commission on Children and Youth car across the overpass above the expressway and down Woodrow Wilson. I slapped the horn, and a minute later Robert walked out, blinking and sullen. He was wearing a dirty white sweater. I tossed my sweater at him. He pulled it on and adjusted it carefully around his neck. I nosed onto the Lodge Expressway and headed north. Robert slid down low in the seat.

"I don't want to see this movie," he said. "I don't want to see no *Romeo and Juliet*."

"You're going to like it."

"I don't want to see no *Romeo and Juliet*."

The theater was in a shopping center. The line to the box office was all white. There were a lot of kids, girls in loafers and tall skinny boys chewing gum and wearing high school letter jackets. They all looked like advertisements for frozen orange juice and Dial soap.

Robert surveyed the line. He looked as though he could have picked up one of those high school basketball stars and snapped him over his knee. "I ain't gettin out of the car," he said.

I parked and got out.

"I ain't gettin out," Robert said.

"Come on, Robert," I said.

His eyes narrowed. He glared up and down the line. He got out.

We stood silently in line. In front of us a couple of girls chatted about a pajama party. "Groovy," one of them said. I bought the tickets and we went in. It was a handsome theater. Naked beams crossed the ceiling of the lobby and the floor was polished brick.

We sat in the last row and the movie began. I recognized the yellow walls and cobbled squares of Verona. I had been there once. Robert sat in the darkness like a chunk of blue granite and watched the movie. Then Romeo killed Tybalt. Robert leaned toward me and whispered, "Is Romeo gonna get killed?"

"Wait," I said.

"Come on, now," he said. I just smiled. "Damn," he muttered. Romeo found Juliet asleep in the tomb. Robert leaned forward and put his chin on the back of the seat in front of him.

"Romeo gonna kill himself," he whispered. "Ain't this something?"

Three girls in front of us were sobbing when the lights came on. You could hear them sniffling all over the theater.

"God*damn*," Robert murmured. He followed me through the crowd out into the brilliant afternoon. "When can we see this picture again?"

"Anytime."

"How come you didn't cry?"

"I'm used to it," I said. "I've seen it before and I've read it."

"Where'd you read it?"

"High school and college."

"So you knew how it was gonna end?"

"Sure."

We got into the car and I headed south on the expressway.

"I ain't gonna lie," Robert said. "I almost cried."

"Nothing wrong with that," I said. "That means you understood it."

"You got to be hip to understand a picture like that," he said.

Larry Phillips was standing with his hands on his hips and his head thrust forward. A flock of girls was gathered around him. They studied the floor. "All right," Larry was saying, "did you see anyone in here? Could anyone have done it while you were here?" The girls stared at the floor. The librarian looked at the ceiling and closed his eyes. "All right," he said. "Go to your next class."

"What happened?" I asked. The girls were filing out quietly.

"Someone stole ten dollars out of a pocketbook."

I had a group that hour. I was sitting on my tabletop trying to teach math when Robert walked in with Larry like an angry dog at his heels. Robert was wearing his coat and a fur hat; he spun and faced the librarian.

Larry passed him and stood over our table. "From now on," he shouted, "if you want to tutor Simmons, tutor him somewhere else. I don't want him in this library."

Robert stood with his feet planted apart and his head tilted back at an angle.

"What happened?" I said.

"He tryin to say I done somethin I ain't done," Robert snarled.

"I'm not saying you did anything," the librarian bellowed. "All I did was ask you a question and you start yelling that you haven't done anything." He looked at me. "All I did was ask him was he in the library, and he starts yelling that he hasn't done anything."

"Robert," I said, "as soon as the hour's over I'll talk to you." Robert nodded and went out into the hall. I joined him when the hour ended. We waited till the hall was empty.

"Now what's he sayin I did?" Robert demanded. He started to pace, spinning abruptly, prowling back and forth.

"Someone stole ten dollars out of a girl's pocketbook."

"And he sayin I did it?"

"Did you do it?"

"No, I ain't done it," he shrilled.

"All right." He hadn't done it.

Larry bounced out into the hall. "Look, I never said you did anything. I asked you a simple question. I asked were you in the library." He glanced at me. I wouldn't look at him.

"I wasn't in your damn library," Robert said.

"Four people saw you in the library."

"Who?" Robert whirled.

"Oh, no," the librarian said. "Oh, no. I don't want them getting beat up."

"I ain't gonna beat them up," Robert muttered. "I'm just gonna make sure they tell the truth."

"Sure," Larry said.

I was sitting on the window ledge. "Hey," I said. "He didn't take the money."

Larry seemed about to shout, then checked it and started in a lower key. "I didn't say he did. I asked him a simple question and he keeps lying. So I don't want him in the library. Then there won't be any problem."

Robert faced him, feet spread. "All right. Fuck it. I'll stay out of your library. Fuck it."

Larry flounced in and slammed the door.

"I'll see if I can get this straightened out," I said. "Listen, he's fair and you know it. He doesn't *want* to think you did it."

"Forget it." Robert went to the windows and gazed into the gray winter light at the houses beyond the parking lot. "Mr. Hough," he murmured, "you don't know what it's like, gettin accused of somethin you ain't done."

"I'm sorry," I said.

"You ain't got no idea what it's like."

He walked off, rolling on the outsides of this heels, his arms swinging easily.

An hour later they found the kid who had taken the money. I went to Robert's home to tell him, but he wasn't there.

"He cares for you and he can't stand to care for you," my mother's letter said. I was having trouble with Robert.

He complained that we were reading too much white man's writing. I gave him an anthology of black poetry. He said he didn't like poetry. I gave him *Soul on Ice*. He said he didn't like it. I gave him *Native Son*. He said he didn't like it. I would give him a book and he would bring it back the next day and drop it on the table like an empty matchbox. "All we ever do is read," he said.

Sometimes he wouldn't come in. I would find him in the hall hunched on the window ledge, gazing out across the rooftops. I would sidle up like a mother trying to persuade her child to take his medicine. Robert wouldn't look at me. "Let's get to work," I would say cheerfully. Sometimes he sighed loudly and scuffed into the room. Sometimes he said he would come in a minute and then he would leave the building.

One day he brought his friend Ron. Ron lived across the street from Robert on Woodrow Wilson, and I often saw him on the street. Robert brought him to school now and then. Ron walked into Mrs. Brooks's room with a transistor radio clutched against his ear. He and Robert sat down in a corner and began to play soul music. Mrs. Brooks was teaching. Her classes were always quiet, and she spoke softly. I walked over.

"Let's get to work."

They looked up at me. Ron was grinning. He had a salmon-colored lower lip and slanted eyes that made him look sinister.

"Damn," Robert said. "I just got here."

"It's your hour now," I said.

He got up slowly and flashed a smile at Ron.

"Turn off the radio," I said.

"Man," Robert said.

Ron clicked off the music and Robert and I went to our table. He had written a paper, and I started to talk about it. Robert sat across from me with his arms folded on his chest. Across the room the static blare of soul music began again.

"Ron, turn it off, will you?"

"Sorry," he said, grinning like a Chinaman. The music stopped. Mrs. Brooks was pretending not to notice.

I went back to the paper. The music started. It was softer this time, and I pretended not to hear it. But it grew louder and louder. I turned. "Come on, Ron. You'd better leave."

"What?"

"Come on. I'll walk down with you so you won't get into any trouble."

"Hey, Mr. Hough," Robert said. Ron got up and

walked out with me. I walked down the stairs with him
and let him out into the March sunlight. Robert was out
in the hall when I got back. He faced me, his hands behind him on the window ledge.

"What'd you throw Ron out for?"

"Because he wouldn't stop playing the radio."

"It ain't enough you on my back," he said. "You got
to get on my friends' backs too."

"What are you talking about?" I said.

"You know what I'm talkin about."

"I've been on your back?"

"Yeah, you've been on my back." He started pacing,
and I sat down. "How come you don't never get after
Taylor and Tut? They your little pets, ain't they?"

"For Christ sake, Robert."

"It's true, though, ain't it?"

"No."

"Hell yes, it's true, and I'm gonna tell you somethin
else." He punched holes in the air with his big index
finger. "Don't let your color go to your head."

My legs had been swinging nervously. They froze.
Robert stuck his hands into his pockets like a prosecutor
who has delivered the final, irrefutable evidence.

I stared at the wooden floor. It was smooth and white
and beginning to warp. "You're my favorite student," I
said.

Robert leaned against the wall and pressed his cheek
against a tin locker. "Sure," he said.

"You really are."

"I wish I could believe that," he murmured.

"I wish you could," I said.

He straightened and buttoned his coat. "I'll see you tomorrow," he said.

He was gone for a week. Then a little girl scampered into Mrs. Brooks's room with a note from the principal.

Will you do something about Robert Simmons? He has been walking all over the building and the teachers are complaining.

I went out and found Robert at our window.

"Say, Robert," I said.

He glanced over his shoulder like a cougar distracted by a noisy bird.

"They want you out of the halls. Want to do some work?"

He started to pace. He rubbed his hard dry palms as though he would strike fire from them. His eyes blazed. He was revved up like a plane straining against the chocks under its wheels. He had been popping pills.

"No, I don't want to do no damn work."

"Then you better leave."

"Why?" He paused in front of me. "I ain't doin nothin."

"I know, but the teachers don't want you in the hall."

"I'm waitin on a friend." His voice was suddenly shrill and husky, as though it were still changing.

"You have to leave," I said. I took his arm and started to lead him down the hall.

"Get your hands off me," he snarled.

I let him go. "Come on, then."

He drifted down the empty hall, pausing at the windows. I trailed like a wary sheepdog. He jogged down the stairs to the landing above the door. He stopped. Another fifteen feet, and he would be out of the building.

"Don't you never grab me again," he said.

"I didn't grab you," I said.

"See, I know why you try to push me around."

"Oh, Jesus."

I knew he wouldn't leave while I was standing there. He was waiting for me to push him. I have a good idea of what is worth a broken nose. It was all right with me if he left after I went upstairs. "I'll see you," I said, and left him on the landing, breathing hard and trembling like a horse who smells smoke.

I thought I had lost Robert. He had needed something I hadn't been able to give; he had been waiting for it. I figured he must have given up.

Every day I passed on the sidewalk beneath the long blank windows of his home. The casings were rotting and it looked dark inside. I wanted to push open the door with the bent coathanger and go up. But I stayed on the sidewalk like a paralytic at the bottom of a staircase, and gazed up at the blank windows.

A Peck of Salt

April. The rancid smells in the alleys thawed and drifted out onto Woodrow Wilson. Robert came back to school. He wasn't high. He wasn't hostile. He sat down across from me and stretched.

"Where you been?" I said.

He shrugged. "I been busy."

"How's Sharon?"

"She's okay."

"Well, look," I said. "Two more months of school. You got to do some work."

He smiled.

"I've about given up the hope of finding something you want to read. And I was planning to have you reading Shakespeare by this time."

He glanced up. "I can read Shakespeare."

"It takes a while to get used to Shakespeare," I said. "We were going to work up to it."

"Shit, I can read it right now."

"It won't be as easy as seeing *Romeo and Juliet*," I said.

"I can read it."

"Let's try it, then."

That afternoon I bought a paperback of *Macbeth*.

"You ought to be proud of him," I told Sharon one day. Robert was holding the book open with one hand and stroking Sharon's leg under the table with the other.

"He's smart, ain't he?" Sharon said.

"Look what he can read," I said.

We finished *Macbeth* two days before the end of school.

Spring deepened to summer. Soul music rolled out of open doors and charged the air over the warm sidewalks. Porches were clogged like overloaded lifeboats. Convertible tops were down.

Robert and I sat in the shade on the school steps. "Are you gonna be here next year?" he said.

"I don't think so."

"Why not?"

"Well, because this is a one-year program. My term ends."

"Why don't you sign up again?"

"Well, I don't know. I haven't thought about it."

"Why don't you stay here, man?"

"There'll be someone to take my place," I said.

"He won't be no good. He won't talk to me like you do."

"Sure he will. He'll be the same as I am."

"What if he ain't?"

"You don't need me," I said. "You have confidence in yourself now."

"I ain't got that much confidence."

"You'll do all right," I said. "I'm not worried."

He looked at me. "You sure? You sure I'll do all right?"

I nodded. A gang of kids was playing baseball on the

empty lot across the street. Robert and I sat silently and watched them. We sat there for twenty minutes. Robert lit a cigarette and stood up.

"Wish I was as sure as you," he said.

EIGHT

"ALL RIGHT," Willie Thomas said. "Let's hear your idea." He leaned back in the swivel chair.

"We'll tie in with summer school," I said. I was seated in front of his desk. "I'll hire ten tutors. We'll have our own reading classes. Big kids teaching little ones."

The Commission on Children and Youth was helping operate the summer Neighborhood Youth Corps. We were using federal money. Agencies all over the city were finding jobs for ghetto kids. The Commission was arranging jobs at hospitals, welfare offices, and recreation centers. Willie had told me to engineer something at the school.

"Here's the thing," I said. "Here's what's going to make this such an exciting program." Willie smiled as though I were a child bride planning a dinner party. "The tutors I hire will be my students. Robert Simmons. Taylor Smith. I'm not going to hire A and B students. Anyone can do that. I'm going to hire the tough ones."

"Why?"

"It'll work two ways. The big ones will teach the little ones to read. The job will make the big ones responsible. They'll be teachers. They'll be constructive members of society."

"If it works."

"It'll work."

You had to be poor to join the Neighborhood Youth Corps. If there were three in your family and the annual income was more than $2,500, you were too rich to qualify. If there were six in your family and the income was more than $4,200, you were too rich. You were too rich if there were nine in your family and you made more than $5,800 a year.

The word spread. Kids flooded Mrs. Brooks's room to see me about jobs.

Most of them had never worked. They were fourteen and fifteen. They had to have money. They needed clothes. They needed movie tickets. They needed radios for the music that beat the rhythm of their lives. They needed reefers from the man on the corner. They needed beer and wine. Without these things, there was nothing more than the baking, cindery streets and the stinking tenement halls.

I chose my tutors like a coach picking an all-star team. I discussed the job with them in private. "If you play around," I said, "you aren't just playing around with yourself. You're hurting these children who want to learn to read." They would nod grimly and I would say, "Can I count on you?" Yes, they would say. I put together a staff of dropouts, juvenile offenders, and school discipline nightmares.

I told them to keep quiet. But the word got out and I was besieged by the jobless. Some of them came from families too rich to qualify. George Bucknell, my basketball player, was one. George's father made a couple of thousand more than the minimum. George and I went to five employment agencies. None could find him a job. He wanted to work at a playground. Basketball was his greatest love, and I had seen him spend hours helping Mrs. Brooks's children learn to read. But no playground could use him. He hung around awhile, then went to his cousin's in Monroe.

Most of the kids who came to me were poor enough. I had to tell them that all the jobs were taken. For two weeks there was a rush. I called Willie and asked him if I could send them to him, but the Commission already had more applicants than jobs. There were hundreds of kids below the poverty line, unable to find work. They would have many steaming hours to pass on the streets that summer.

"How come you hire him and not me, man?" I was asked.

"I can only hire ten," I would answer.

"But why can't I be one of the ten?"

They told me of families of ten and twelve, of mothers on welfare or working for seventy-five dollars a week. They wanted to work for eight weeks, twenty-six hours a week, at a dollar thirty-five an hour. But there wasn't enough money to pay them.

Meanwhile, the government was getting ready to put the first men on the moon.

Robert's girl friend Sharon was seven months pregnant. Her child blossomed under her cotton frock. Sharon's hair was washed and set and her face was tastefully powdered. She asked me for a job.

"Are you going to be strong enough?" I asked.

She nodded, her eyes lowered. She seemed to have known a hundred pregnancies. I hired her.

I didn't want to have to explain a pregnant tutor to the social workers in the office of the Mayor's Committee on Human Resources Development, so I took Sharon's sister Linda to register for Sharon. Linda looked like the gangling embryo of a lady on a Spanish bullfight poster. She had copper skin and jet eyebrows. Someday she would be rounded and feline.

We climbed the stairs to the city office on Woodward Avenue. "Remember," I said. "You're Sharon." Linda had Sharon's birth certificate and social security card in her purse.

"I'm Sharon," she said.

The office was low-ceilinged and hot. Electric fans whirred. The staff sat at long tables covered with stacks of applications. They were young and looked intelligent. Most of them were black. The room was full of kids. They sat at old school desks filling out applications, bent over and dragging their pencils along the mazes of lines and boxes. Most of them were boys. All were black. I had gone through this with all my tutors.

A black girl with Afro hair handed Linda the cards and sheets at the reception desk. Linda picked her way to an empty desk. I leaned against the wall and watched her fill out the forms. When she had finished, she walked over to the long tables. A young man with a natural told her to sit down. He checked her papers, then asked some questions. Linda looked him in the eye and answered. I watched nervously. It lasted five minutes.

"How was it?"

"Cool," she said.

Sharon had the job.

I composed a letter to parents. I typed it on a stencil and ran hundreds of copies on the mimeograph machine. Here it is:

DEAR PARENT,

This summer, through each summer school day, there will be special reading classes.

Mr. Hough, who has been tutoring all year, will be in charge of the program. Tutors will be neighborhood boys and girls of the Neighborhood Youth Corps, trained by Mr. Hough.

Your child will get personal, expert attention. It will cost nothing. If your child is enrolled in summer school, he can be tutored during his free hour.

A Peck of Salt

If you are interested, write your name and your child's name below, and have your child return the form to Mr. Hough.

Special reading classes. Personal, expert attention. I believed it all. The forms came back by the dozen.

Car horns trumpeted the explosion of summer. Radio station WJLB spread Junior Walker and Stevie Wonder on shimmering waves. The heat trapped the smells of beer and exhaust and pinned them at eye level. Teachers locked their classrooms and went to the mountains.

I unlocked Mrs. Brooks's room and opened the windows. Mrs. Brooks had left me everything. Storybooks lined the shelves. The closets held reading texts for every elementary grade level. There were pencils. There were crayons. The tables and desks were neatly placed. The blackboards were scrubbed.

The sky looked as solid as the side of a polished Cadillac. The Sears Building shot up, flashing the temperature, the time, the temperature. Eighty-five and eight fifteen.

The tutors and students started to drift in at eight thirty. The children sat down quietly and stared at the blank blackboard. The tutors collected at the window and talked. I checked the tentative schedule I had made, and started ordering tutors to work. When I called his name, a tutor would say a few more words to the group

at the window, smile, and saunter over to me. I would
introduce him to the child. They would pick a book at
the back of the room and sit side by side. Some tutors
took two or three children. Now and then a mother
brought her child, explaining how the child had fallen
behind and how much he needed extra help. By nine,
everyone was working. At nine-thirty the bell rang. The
children scattered, and a fresh flock wandered in.

I appointed Robert Simmons assistant principal. I figured it would be like asking him to read Hemingway
and *Macbeth;* ask more and you got it.

"Read, boy, 'fore I smack you!"
The child bolted up out of his chair. Bennie lunged at
him and missed. The little boy ran into the hall, sobbing.
I caught him halfway down the stairs. I knelt and
mopped his face with my handkerchief. "Come on," I
said. "You can read with someone else. Do you want to
read with someone else?"
He nodded. I led him back. Bennie glowered at him.
"No more of that," I said to Bennie. I took the child to
Sharon. She was working with another little boy. "Can
you handle one more?" She nodded. "Be gentle," I said.
She nodded again. The child sat down and started to
read.
Sandra, my other girl tutor, made the second rescue
that first day. There was a crack that made everyone
look up. William had slammed a book on the desktop
under the chin of a plump little girl. She stood up and

hid her face in her hands and cried. Sandra jumped up and led the little girl out into the hall. They came back a few minutes later.

"Fat little pig," William muttered.

"You keep quiet," I snapped. William leaned back and smiled. He had to appear in court in a couple of weeks on a breaking and entering charge. "You're getting paid not to talk like that," I said.

"Okay, man."

School ended at twelve thirty, "Starting tomorrow," I announced, "we'll have a meeting every day after school. You're getting paid till one thirty, you're going to stay till one thirty." They started out.

"One more thing," I said. "Your first checks won't be here till the end of the second week." They shrugged. The room emptied. I didn't think about it again.

Robert looked like a good assistant principal. He prowled among the tutors, pinning them with baleful stares. They didn't like it. But they were stuck.

Robert and Sharon had a quarrel in the middle of the second day. There was a sudden, almost wordless eruption, and I hear Robert snap, "Don't you say no more, goddamn it." I went over and whispered that I didn't want him to swear in front of the children. He glared over my shoulder at Sharon. I straightened and turned. Suddenly Sharon scurried out the door. Robert shot after her. I left them alone. Twenty minutes later they came back together, sullen and silent. Sharon's students had waited for her.

At the meeting after school I lectured about some techniques of teaching reading. They stared out at the cloudless sky. They yawned. I sent them home at one and followed Robert to the door. The school was still. The other teachers and students had gone home at twelve-thirty. I called Robert and he stopped and leaned against the wall.

"Look," I said. "Solve your domestic problems out of school, will you?"

"Don't worry," he said. "I ain't gonna run after her no more."

"And stop saying things that make her run."

"Don't worry, Mr. Hough."

Sharon came carefully down the stairs. She didn't look at Robert.

"I was just saying that you two have to stop this stuff," I said.

"All right," she said. She walked out, ignoring Robert. She had to waddle to carry her baby.

Robert peered out the window as Sharon passed on the dusty white street. "See you tomorrow," he muttered. He darted out and I saw him chase her and catch her on Twelfth Street. They walked out of sight together. I went home.

Up the stairs and around the corner chugged the school principal. He was wearing a plaid shirt. His neck was pink. He was smiling apologetically.

"Can I speak to you?" he said.

I was out in the hall. Some of the tutors had dragged desks and chairs out there. They were strewn around at odd angles, each with a child at his side. I followed the principal down half a flight to a landing. The principal put his hands in his pockets.

"Hiring Robert Simmons and Sharon Shipley was a mistake," he began. He sliced the air tentatively with a flat hand, as though he were afraid he would hit something.

"What do you mean?" I said.

"Hiring her in her condition was a mistake."

"She's doing a fine job." Sharon worked with three little girls. They wouldn't read for anyone else. After school she took their hands and led them down to the door.

"But don't you see?" the principal said. "She used to go to this school."

"So what?"

"The board of education has a policy regarding girls in her condition."

"My program has nothing to do with the board of education," I said.

"Yes, but it does take place in the school." He smiled tightly. "Even the community women are complaining." There were volunteer women helping some of the teachers. They were all old and well fed. They looked like matriarchal hens. "And quite frankly," the principal went on, "a girl that age has no business getting pregnant." The smile became a grimace. "Think how much it costs. Damn it, I'm a taxpayer."

I stared out the window. The sun glinted on shards of glass on the asphalt. *You son of a bitch.* I should have done or said something valorous. But I stared out at the playground. I had never been a hero.

"So what are you saying?" I said.

"I'm saying this has to be Sharon's last day."

"Her last day?"

"John, you're very liberal. You're very idealistic. But you don't take into consideration all the . . ."

"So you won't let her in the school?"

"I can't." I felt like smashing those glasses against his face. "Would you like me to talk to her?" he offered.

"No. I want to talk to her."

"Would you like me to talk to Mr. Thomas?"

"Forget it," I said. "I'll take care of it."

I went to find Mrs. Davis. Mrs. Davis was the Community Agent. Her job was to link the school with the neighborhood. We were pretty good friends.

"You got to help me," I said.

She already knew all about it. "The community won't stand for it," she said. About six old women seemed to have become the community.

"What if I refuse to fire Sharon?"

"You can't. The school is community property." I felt double-crosssed. "Want me to talk to Sharon?" Mrs. Davis offered.

"Why doesn't anyone think I can talk to Sharon? You think I got a speech defect or something?"

"No, John," she soothed, putting her hand on my shoulder like a mother. "I can explain it to her. It's hard for you to understand what it means, having a pregnant girl in school like that. I been around longer than you."

Bullshit. "I'll explain it fine," I said.

I waited till everyone had gone. Robert was sitting on a table with his arm around Sharon. I told them what had happened. "I'm sorry," I said. "I'm truly sorry."

"That's all right," Robert said. His eyes were slitted. Sharon didn't move or look at me. She only smiled, a tainted angel. Robert slapped her thigh. "Come on, old lady," he said. They strolled out.

I telephoned Willie Thomas that afternoon. "What do you think about fighting it?" I asked.

There was a pause on the other end. "They kind of have us," Willie said. "They could blow the whole program." There was another silence. "And it could be nasty for Sharon. It could be very nasty."

"It's the idea of it," I said.

"Let's forget it and teach those kids to read."

Next morning as school was beginning and the children were straggling up the stairs, the principal bustled in. "I have to talk to you," he announced.

I followed him into the hall.

"Did you leave with Simmons yesterday?" the principal demanded.

"I don't remember."

I had left Robert and Sharon and their friend Sonny leaning against the wall beside the school door. They had been smoking cigarettes. They had nodded at me as I came out.

"Well, he broke my windshield." The principal squinted at me through his glasses as though he expected me to black out. "Two rocks, right through the glass. I found them on the front seat. Right there sitting on the front seat."

A delicious purr trilled through me. I said nothing.

"It's going to cost me ninety-seven dollars," he said. "That's almost a hundred dollars."

"How do you know it was Robert?" I asked.

"Of course it was. This is a typical Simmons stunt."

"So what do you want me to do?" I asked.

"Walk those people off the school grounds." I had thought he was going to tell me to fire Robert. "If this happens again, Simmons is going to get the axe too."

I was looking out the window. At that moment Robert, Sharon, and Sonny walked past on their way to the door. They were spread in jaunty single file, Robert in the lead. The principal saw them. "Okay," I said, and headed down the stairs to intercept them. I got there as they walked in.

"Who busted the windshield?"

They stared at me. Sonny snickered like a squirrel.

"Did someone do that?" Sharon said. "About time someone did that." She smiled and her eyes rolled. She was high.

"Funny thing," I said to Robert. "He thinks you did it."

"Me?" Robert pointed at his own heart and stuck out his head. Sonny was still snickering.

"It's all right," I said. "He's not going to do anything. I just want to know who did it."

"It wasn't me," Robert said.

"Who was it?"

"You promise you won't tell?"

"You know I won't tell," I said.

Robert raised his big hand and punched his index finger at Sharon. She smiled. The Madonna with the Rock. Just then the principal passed. He avoided looking at any of us and scuttled by wordlessly. Robert and Sharon watched him. No one spoke until he was gone.

"Whose idea was it?" I asked.

"Sonny's." Robert grinned. I could picture it.

"No more," I said. "No more, or this whole thing's finished. None of us will have jobs."

"Okay," Robert said.

He and Sonny started up the stairs. Sharon watched them from the bottom. "I'll be at your house," she called.

"Cool," Robert said.

I trailed them to the room. The temperature had gone up over ninety.

Sonny lived with his brother, sister, aunt and grandmother above a dry cleaner's on Woodrow Wilson. His aunt worked at a bank. His sister was a little girl and his brother went to high school. Sonny had once gone to our school, but for two years he had been at a special school for boys. He had a tough, lumpy face and a chip out of his front tooth. He wasn't big. He reminded me of a badger.

He used to come to school with Robert. I had never had any trouble with him, but I heard that his history was a long war with teachers. He had worked for several years as a shoeshine boy in the barrooms along Woodrow Wilson. I used to see him sometimes on my way to school. He would be leaning against the wall beside the door to a bar, one arm straight against the wall, one leg bent. He wore old pants and sneakers.

"Why don't you hire Sonny?" Robert had said when I was planning the program. I wanted tutors like Sonny. I was going to make them constructive members of society. I hired Sonny in the Simmons's living room.

He and Robert and Mrs. Simmons and I were sitting around on the tattered furniture and I was explaining the job to Sonny. "Think you can do it?"

"I can do it all right," Sonny said. He had a nervous, husky voice and he talked very fast. He was sitting bent forward with his hands on his knees.

"I'll tell you what," Mrs. Simmons said. "Sonny gets up in the morning. Yes sir, he be there on time in the morning."

"I'll wake Robert up," Sonny said.

"You got the job," I said.

So Sonny had joined us.

NINE

"YOU SHOULD have told me," I said.

Willie Thomas folded his hands on his desk blotter. "I thought I made it clear."

"You said they were getting paid at the end of the second week."

"No, it was always going to be the end of the third week." They weren't getting three weeks' pay, either. They were getting a week's pay. The rest would come at the end of the summer.

"My God," I said. "Those kids are going to kill me."

Next day I decided to tell them at the meeting after school.

At eleven Robert and Sonny wandered out of the room. They went down to the basement to smoke. The janitor found them down there. They were sitting on a pile of chairs, swinging their legs and smoking. "Hey," the janitor said. They hopped down. Sonny looked at the janitor and carefully kicked the pile. Several chairs clattered to the floor. The janitor told Sonny to pick them up. Sonny told the janitor to do something to himself. The janitor ordered them both to the office. Sonny told him what to do to himself again and he and Robert walked out of the building.

"Tough kids," the janitor told me. "That light-skinned one got a lot of mouth."

Robert and Sonny didn't come back. I shouldn't have announced that the money wasn't coming till they were there. The children went home. We cleaned the room and sat down.

"I have some bad news," I said. They froze. They knew it was about the money. "You're not getting paid until the end of next week."

They stared at me. *"Shee-*it," someone whistled.

"And that isn't all," I said.

William was sitting up front. "Just tell us we ain't get-tin our three weeks' pay," he said.

"You're not," I said. "You're getting a one week check."

They gaped at me. Three weeks' pay would have been ninety dollars. Most of them had never seen more than twenty dollars at a time. They were going to get thirty after working for three weeks.

"Listen," I said. "I have no control over this money. It's government money. It comes from Washington. There isn't anything I can do about it." Perspiration slid down my forehead into my eyebrows.

"Okay, baby," William said. He sat up straight. "I just want to know one thing. You told Robert and Sonny yet?"

"No."

William smiled a wicked smile. "I want to see you tell Robert and Sonny. I just want to see it."

"Don't worry about it," I said.

I perspired walking home. There was no mail in the box on the porch. I called Larry.

"Let's go have a beer," I said.

"What's the matter?"

"Nothing," I said. "I just feel like talking."

"All right."

We went to the Trade Winds. Bill wasn't there. He sang three nights a week. I ordered two beers. We watched the frothy heads surge to the rims of the glasses.

"What's the matter?" Larry asked.

"I don't know."

Someone played "Good Morning, Starshine" on the jukebox. It was gay and vibrant. It reminded me of a summer morning in a countryside of forests and pastures.

"I feel as though suddenly it's too much for me," I said.

"What do you mean?" he said.

"I've always been able to handle things. I don't know if I can handle this. They're going to erode me." *Good morning, starshine . . .* I could see the early sun boring through a canopy of leaves, touching thick, wet grass. "Right down to nothing," I said.

"Listen," he said. "I'll tell you something about you. You're a very intense person, you know? You're wound up. You're wound up all the time."

Right down to nothing. Melted.

"Relax. It's no big thing."

The song trailed off and ended. "I'd love to relax," I said. Suddenly I knew I wouldn't relax till I got home. I tried to ignore this, but it stayed, wedged in my consciousness.

"It's no big thing," Larry said. He ordered two more beers.

"My last one," I said.

"At ten o'clock?"

"I'm pretty tired," I said.

Next day Robert and Sonny didn't show until ten. I was in the hall reading with Jamie. We had so many children that I had begun to double as tutor. Robert and Sonny ambled up the hall. Their eyes were half closed. They looked like sleepy barracuda. They stopped in front of me and I got up. They knew all about the money.

"Where'd you go yesterday?" I said.

They stared at me. Sonny hopped up onto the window ledge. Robert started his nervous, whirling ramble. He rubbed his hands together. His face was a jagged shadow.

I closed the book and told Jamie to go into the room and wait for me. He lingered in the doorway. Jamie never missed anything. I folded my arms and took a deep breath.

"What's this about us not gettin paid Friday?" Robert growled.

"The money won't be in," I said. Who had told them? "I can't get it. There's nothing I can do about it."

"Ain't that a bitch?" Robert snarled, spinning. "We workin for nothin."

"You're not working for nothing," I said. "You'll be paid for every hour you work."

"When? When the whole damn program is over?"

Sonny stayed perched on the window ledge. He looked like a cranky, ruffled owl. Robert paced. I felt as though the world were spinning faster and faster and leaving me behind.

"Anybody who works for nothin is a fool."

"If I could get the money, I'd get it," I said. I would have swum the Detroit River for that money.

"Shee-it," Robert hissed. "If you wanted that money, you could get it."

"Would you like to talk to Mr. Thomas?" I offered.

"Shit. So he can tell me more lies?"

"Who's telling lies?"

"You, baby, you."

William had come out. He had jumped up onto the window ledge beside Sonny. He was watching me, smiling hungrily. I knew who had told Robert about the money.

"You're talking like a fool," I said.

"And you lyin about the money."

"All right, goddamn it, you're not getting paid Friday, and if you don't like it, too damn bad." The words tumbled out. The children had heard me. They spilled out into the hall.

Robert spun once more and faced me, fifteen feet away. "You better have my money Friday."

"I'm not going to have your money Friday."

"You better."

"What's going to happen if I don't?"

William sniggered.

"You'll see," Robert said. He lowered his voice. "And it might happen tonight."

"Fine," I said. "I'll be watching out."

The children were gazing at me. The tutors were smiling softly. "Back in the room," I said. My mouth was parched. There was a reluctant withdrawal. "Get in the room, William." He dropped off the hall window ledge and sauntered in. Robert sat down in one of the desks in the hall and glared at the ceiling.

I went in and returned to the book with Jamie. My insides felt like slush. The phrases and pictures in Jamie's book seemed to recede. I focused on them and they receded again. I spotted Taylor Smith doing nothing and asked him to work with Jamie. I went back into the hall.

Robert was hunched like a bronze statue on the desktop. Sonny still roosted on the window ledge. It was quiet out there, as though a big wind had swept through the corridor and then died.

"Can I say something to you?" I said softly.

"I ain't stoppin you."

He stood up. His legs were rigid, his hands were rammed into his pockets. *He cares for you, and he can't stand to care for you.*

"I just want to tell you that it really bothers me to see you mad at me like this." I leaned on the window ledge and stared down across the parking lot. Sonny was sitting beside me. He didn't look at me. "Makes me wonder where I went wrong."

Robert stood still. He blinked. His eyes opened a little wider. Sonny began to hum softly. I went into the room.

That night I had to force myself to eat. I lay down and listened to the Tigers game. They were playing Cleveland. Ken Harrelson of Cleveland hit two home runs. Harrelson had long golden hair. He wore bell-bottom pants and sequined jackets. They called him "The Hawk." When he had arrived in Cleveland in a trade, a crowd had met him at the airport and two beauty queens had placed a wreath around his neck. He could hit, too.

I fell asleep at about nine.

Robert was grim and closed next day. He patroled the room ferociously. I left him in charge and took a student into the stillness of the hall. The sun bore down through the wide-open windows. We opened *The Cat in the Hat*.

"God*damn*." It popped out of the room. There was a

flurry of words. A chair crashed. I got up and went in.

Taylor Smith was standing in the middle of the room pointing at Sonny. Sonny was sprawled on a chair at the back. Robert stood behind the teacher's desk at the front. Taylor looked at one, then the other.

Taylor didn't need money as badly as the others. He was making spending cash in the drug business. Still, I had invited him to work with us. He had considered it for two days, and accepted.

"I saw you do it," Sonny was saying.

Taylor's hands were held away from his body. He had big hands and strong wrists. "I don't give a fuck what you saw!"

There were little children all over the room. *Tutors will be neighborhood boys and girls trained by Mr. Hough. Your child will get personal, expert attention.*

"Shit," Taylor muttered.

Robert glared at him from one side, Sonny from the other. I went over and put my hand on his shoulder. "You all right?" I said.

He shrugged as though he were clearing a knot out of his shoulder muscle. "I tell you what," he said. "We'll drop it. We just won't say no more about it." He kicked a chair out from a table and sat down. They left him alone. I never found out what had happened.

"Let's get back to work," I said.

"Tell him, Sonny." It was Robert from the front of the room.

A Peck of Salt

"Okay, Hough," Sonny chirped. He grinned like an evil monkey. Robert snorted into his hand.

I looked at Sonny. "Okay, *Mr.* Hough," I corrected. The room got quiet. Drops of sweat from under my arms ran in two cool streaks down my flanks. "Okay, *Mr.* Hough," I repeated into the silence.

Sonny grinned. "Then you call me Mr. Lamson," he said.

"No, you call me Mr. Hough," I said.

He shrugged. "Okay, Mr. Hough."

I turned my back on him and fell into a chair.

The morning wore on. The children went home. We straightened the room. As we were sitting down for the meeting, Sharon walked in. She and Robert glanced at each other. She sat down quietly off to the side.

I wiped my forehead and neck with my handkerchief. They sat calmly in front of me. None of them looked hot.

"Let's forget the meeting today," I said.

They scattered. Sharon and Robert and Sonny lingered behind and strolled down the hall. I locked the room and followed them out. Robert was silent and listless. I felt whipped. Robert and Sharon crossed Woodrow Wilson without speaking to me. I continued with Sonny to the door to his home.

"See you tomorrow," he said.

The gutter was littered with papers and broken glass. The brick buildings looked more grimy than ever. It wasn't even July yet. Time inched along, as though mired in the heat that had lodged in the streets and alleys.

The temperature held at a blistering plateau. The humidity climbed. Robert and Sonny kept straying from the room. I would find them in the basement or outside on the steps. They would glance at me like heavyweights at a featherweight who keeps insisting he wants to fight. I would tell them to go to the room and they would say nothing. Their eyes would narrow a little more. I would leave them, and a few minutes later they would scuff into the room.

Some of the tutors, especially Sonny, were rough with the children. I could stop that, but I had to see it. A few of the children weren't coming any more.

We pushed on toward the end of the second week. I got a phone call at school. It was Willie.

"You have two boys who aren't certified," he said. "Bring them over here right away so they can sign and be certified."

"Who are they?"

"Robert Simmons and Sonny Lamson."

The office of the Commission on Children and Youth was dark and filled with the hum and breeze of electric fans. Robert and Sonny stood by a desk while a secretary shuffled through papers looking for the ones they had to sign. They were still registering and processing the Neighborhood Youth Corps. The office was cluttered with half-completed forms. Several kids sat on the chairs along the wall. Their wrists hung from their knees, their heads were bowed. The girl found Robert's and Sonny's papers and pushed them forward on the desk. Robert studied his and signed. Sonny signed.

"They know when they're getting paid?" the girl said. She was a bony girl with a natural.

"Sure," I said. "Next week."

"No, the week after," she said. "They're just getting certified, so they won't be on the payroll till the week after."

I groped for the wall behind me. Robert and Sonny stood frozen in front of the desk.

"But your others are certified," the girl said cheerfully. "They'll be paid at the end of next week." My mind raced back. Robert and Sonny had been the last I had taken to register at the office on Woodward.

Willie had heard us. He came out of his office. "I explained that," he said.

"My God, Willie," I said. "I thought it was all set." I fell back against the wall. The fans sang, blowing hot air like a desert breeze.

"No," Willie said. "You had to have them certified by the end of last week." There were two hundred kids who had taken jobs through this office. Willie didn't have time to worry about two of my tutors.

"I thought they were certified." I didn't even know what it meant to be certified. The formalities were many and baffling.

Willie calculated Robert. "You understand, don't you?" he said. It was plain that Robert understood nothing.

"Isn't there anything I can do?" I was pleading.

"I'm afraid not," Willie said. "The money's in Washington."

I waved good-bye bravely. Robert and Sonny clattered wordlessly down the narrow staircase. We stepped out onto the hot white sidewalk.

"Fuck this job," Robert said.

The children had gone and the tutors were sitting around waiting for us. Robert had sat still in the car on the way back. Now his anger detonated. He lurched to the center of the room. The tutors watched uneasily.

"If you all want to work for nothin, go ahead," Robert snarled.

They shot up. "You're all getting paid next week," I said. They sat down. They didn't look at Robert. They didn't want to argue with him, but they didn't care to join him. Money takes the edge off the spirit of revolution.

"Let's go home," I said.

Bennie and William and a couple others were throwing a rubber ball back and forth. They pranced around tossing it to each other, bouncing it off the wall. *We didn't dig Robert's rap, but we ain't your boys neither.* I had to take them one by one and shove them out of the room. I did it as playfully as I could. They drifted down the hall. Robert and Sonny left about five minutes after everyone else.

I lingered, picking up pencils, shelving books, aligning chairs and desks. It looked like the site of a brawl in there. I picked up one of Mrs. Brooks's posters. It had a shoeprint on it. The fire alarm went off.

It ripped into the silence, a wailing, hysterical buzz that bolted up and down the halls. I collected the pencils and put them in a box. I wrapped rubber bands around the stacks of flash cards. The fire alarm gave a final raucous howl. Silence.

The principal and several teachers were holding council on the steps outside. Fifty feet away Robert and Sonny were lolling against the wall, smoking cigarettes.

"John, did Simmons pull that alarm?" the principal said.

"I don't know," I said. "They all left fifteen minutes ago."

The principal looked at me as though I were someone else's naughty child. It would be awkward to spank me, but he was starting to consider it.

I walked over to Robert and Sonny. They blew smoke out of their mouths and squinted at me.

"Someone pulled the alarm," I said.

"Ain't that too bad?" Robert said.

"Yes," I said. "It is."

I went home and fell asleep. I slept the rest of the

afternoon. The next day was quiet. Robert and Sonny didn't come until ten thirty. They left an hour later. I wrote their hours on the time sheet, so they wouldn't get paid for the hours they didn't work. Everyone else seemed tired. Their attention wandered, across the room or out the window. I had to bring them back.

The weekend came. I think I went to a movie. It was like going to sleep Friday afternoon and waking up Monday morning. I came back for the third week.

A crowd had collected in the hall. Robert and Sonny were in the middle of it. Their breaths smelled of beer. The teacher down the hall had stepped out of her room and was yelling at the crowd. She saw me. "They were wrestling," she said, and ducked back into her room.

"Get in the room," I said to Robert.

He cocked his head. "You *always* after me and Sonny." The kids got quiet. "Ain't that a bitch?"

"Get in the room," I said.

"Give me my money," he said. "Give me my goddamn money. Before you be tellin me what to do, you give me my motherfuckin money."

They had me in a corner now. It wouldn't even help to turn around. I picked our kids out of the crowd and sent them into the room. I told the passers-by to keep going. We went into the room.

"Where are the rest of your tutors, Mr. Hough?" Robert taunted.

"With their students."

"But where are they?" He snorted. "You don't even know where the hell they are." He was right. "Your whole program is fallin apart."

I returned to where I had been playing Spill and Spell and picked up the lettered dice. "It's time to go," I said. "We're going home a little early today." They gazed up at me, two little boys, and I put a hand on the shoulder of each and led them to the door. Sandra was surrounded by little girls. She always had a group. I told her to get rid of them.

"We're going to settle it," I told Robert.

"Settle it how?" he snarled. "I'm about through talkin."

"Settle it however you want."

The spinning earth was accelerating again. I couldn't hold on to anything. I sent Taylor to find the other tutors. I waited outside the room. I could hear Robert and Sonny talking about the money. Their voices were rapid and nervous, spattered with obscenities.

The tutors filed ceremoniously into the room. Bennie slammed the door and pulled the shade. Sonny dropped onto a chair, which he tilted and pivoted on one leg. Robert got up on the window ledge, a stark silhouette high against the great panel of bright blue sky.

"All right," I said. "What's the problem?" I was sitting on top of the teacher's desk.

"You know what the problem is," Robert rumbled. "We the only ones not gettin our money. Well, we gonna keep fuckin around till we get our money."

Sonny pivoted his chair. A nervous badger.

"I can't get the money," I said.

"What would you do if you were in our place?" Robert demanded.

"I wouldn't like it," I said. I looked at the Sears Building, way off in the sky. *Twelve thirty-one. Ninety-three.* "What would you do if you were in my place?"

Robert flattened his hand and lifted it in an arc against the sky. "TWA," he said.

The kids guffawed. There was no boredom at this meeting. Sonny's frog-like obscenities mingled with the laughter.

"You know, Sonny, you talk a lot," I said.

The room got still.

"I taught him everything he knows," Robert's voice cut the silence.

"Did you teach him how to talk?" I said.

Robert cocked his fists and jabbed the air with his left, snapped it back and crossed with his right. "Why don't you fire on him, Sonny?" he said softly. "You said you was gonna kick his ass if you didn't get your money."

"That's a good one," I said. Sonny wasn't big enough.

Sonny let his chair settle onto all four legs. Everyone was silent, waiting. Sonny contemplated the desktop like a gambler deciding whether to bet or fold. He stood up. There was a chair near him. He grabbed the chair and hurled it, like an Olympic hammer thrower. The chair bounced off the concrete wall and crashed to the floor. It lay there on its back. It wasn't broken. It had metal legs. Sonny sat down at his desk.

"Okay, Mr. Hough," he said. "I'm cool now." I stared at him. "I got it out of my system." He crossed his legs and scratched his chin. "Tell you what I'm gonna do, Mr. Hough. I'm gonna come to work on time. I'm gonna stop playin around. I'm gonna tutor good, man." He held his palm out as though it held his pet flea. "And then, and then if I don't get paid next Friday, then I *am* gonna kick ass."

"Fair enough," I said.

Robert looked at Sonny as though Sonny had suggested that they all donate their summer's earnings to the PTA. He dropped off the window ledge and prowled across the front of the room. There was a bulletin board propped on a tripod. Robert rested his elbows on it, as though he were leaning on a fence. I swiveled on the desktop.

"How about you?" I said. "You got it out of your system?"

He studied the floor between his elbows. "I ain't got no system."

"What are you going to do?"

"Just what I been doin."

"I want to get everything settled now," I said. "I don't want to go on about the money and I don't want to

chase you all over the school the rest of the summer."
He started pacing, rubbing his palms like two slabs of
flint. "You understand?" I said.

He glanced at me. "What you sayin?"

"You've been saying that if you don't get paid you're
going to kick my ass. All right. You're not going to get
paid. So come kick my ass."

The tutors gave a low, voluptuous moan, the sound
that rolls down from the grandstand when a pitcher
throws one at someone's head. Bennie and William
jumped up and started dragging the desks and chairs
back. They pulled every desk and chair away from the
center of the room, forming an arena. I never saw them
work so fast.

"I ain't playin," Robert said. "You mess with me, you
gonna get fucked up, 'cause I ain't playin."

"Work him over, Mr. Hough," Sonny cackled.

Robert strolled to the desk at the front of the room.
He stopped in front of me and began to peel off his
jersey. It was a gray jersey with cut-off sleeves. He lifted
it over his stomach, over his chest, over his head, and
dropped it like a used napkin on the desk. His torso
looked like wrought iron.

I took my comb and an envelope from my shirt
pocket, keys and change and wallet from my pants. My
mouth was full of ashes.

Robert glided out from behind the desk. The room
was silent. "Now," he said. "You want to fuck with me,
come on."

"You wanted some money from me, remember?"

"Forget the money," he snarled. He was stalking me. The muscles on his shoulders were taut. He looked as though he could have knocked the head off a statue. "You think you're bad, Mr. Hough. You wanted a fight, now you got one. So come on and put your hands on me."

"We're talking about the money," I said.

"Forget the money."

"All right," I said.

I picked up my wallet and comb and keys and change. At least I had offered myself. If he had really wanted me, he could have had me.

"Let's go home," I said. They got up slowly and straggled out, muttering and glancing at me. If they had paid to see it, they would have demanded refunds.

Robert slid into his jersey. I shut the door. Robert stopped a foot from it and stared at it as though it would open by itself.

"What's going on, Robert?" I said. "You wanted me to stay next year, and now we're almost fighting."

"You ask yourself what's going on." He stared at the door.

"I've been asking myself," I said.

"Forget it," he said. He studied the door.

"I don't want to forget it."

The door clicked open and Robert's brother stuck his head in. "Butch is waitin on you," he said.

"He'll be right there," I said.

The door closed. Robert kept watching it.

"Forget it, Mr. Hough. Just please forget it."

I sagged against the wall. I hugged my rib cage and held on as though everything were about to spill out of me. "Go ahead, Robert," I said. "I'll see you tomorrow."

He reached for the doorknob. His face looked drained. I heard his footsteps recede down the hall.

"I have something to say," I announced. The children had gone home. I stood in the middle of the room with my hands on my hips. "This program is a joke."

That morning Robert, Sonny, Bennie, and William had taken a girl named Elaine down to the boys' room in the basement. Elaine was an eighth grader who was taking a math course. She spent a lot of time talking to the boys in the halls. That morning my expert tutors had talked her into going down to the boys' room. They were down there nearly an hour. Later they went back.

"A *joke!*"

They stared at me.

"So the way I see it, there's only one thing to do." I could see the Sears Building. The clock labeled each minute. "We're going to close shop."

"Say which?"

"We're going to close shop. Call it off. Hang it up."

"What for?" Robert said.

"What for?" I said. "What for?" I started to roam

around the arena. "You spend all day in the halls. You want to do everything except what you're getting paid to do. I see you slapping students. I see you smoking outside." I looked at Bennie. He was short and stocky, very clever. "Bennie," I said. "What do you tell me when I tell you to get to work?"

Bennie cracked a guilty smile. "I tell you to get off my back."

"William. What do you tell me?"

William smirked "I tell you what Bennie tells you."

I sat down on top of the desk. I lowered my voice. "And you ask me what for.   Jesus.   *That's* what for."

Robert was sitting on the long table across the room from me. "So I was right yesterday. When I said your program was fallin apart, I was right." His words were spiced with challenge.

"You were right."

His extended arm froze for a second, then sank limply to his lap. "And you was wrong." He said it as though I hadn't heard him the first time.

"I was wrong," I said firmly.

Robert folded his arms across his chest and studied me. His forehead wrinkled. "But you wasn't wrong," he said.

"Oh, yes. I was wrong, all right." I glanced around at them. They were watching me, foreheads creased, chewing gum slowly. "Now if you want to keep working, I can find you other jobs."

"Wait a minute," Bennie said. Everyone started to murmur, and Robert's husky voice rose above the noise and silenced it.

"Be cool."

He hopped off the table and walked slowly to the center of the arena. "Now," he said. "All this talk about how good your tutors was doin, all of it jive, right?"

"I was wrong."

"And what about you tellin Mr. Thomas that you didn't need no help from him?"

"I told him I wanted to *try* to handle it myself."

"You told him you *could* handle it yourself."

I shrugged. "All right. I was wrong again."

Robert stroked his jaw. "It don't make sense, man."

"I didn't know you was a quitter," Bennie said.

"I am."

"Be cool, Bennie," Robert snapped. He stuck his hands into his hip pockets. "Why don't you give us one more chance? See, me and Sonny and Bennie and William, we had a secret today." The secret was Elaine with her pants down in the boys' room.

"Sure," I said. "Every chance you get, you're going to have another secret like that."

Robert fought a smile, and Bennie and Sonny snorted into their hands. "No, we ain't," Robert said.

Taylor Smith was lying on his back across two desks. "Think of it like this, Mr. Hough. You down here where the riots was, tryin to do some good."

"I've failed."

"Wait a minute." Robert pivoted and took a step toward me. "I just got a idea. Since you tired of playin with us I tell you what. Let me be principal. Let me run the show, and you be assistant principal."

I stared out at the thick blue summer sky. In one month I would be home. "You think you can make this program work?"

Robert surveyed the group like a matador inspecting bulls with sawed-off horns. "Shee-it," he said.

"All right," I said. "Starting tomorrow, you're principal. But if things don't get straight, we close shop."

"Cool."

Robert walked with me to Woodrow Wilson. He stopped on the corner. "It don't make sense. I don't get it, Mr. Hough."

"I think I've had it," I said.

"Naw," he said. "I can't believe that. You okay, man."

TEN

"I WANT a new principal," Taylor said. He was slumped on the desk, glowering.

"What?" Robert was standing behind the teacher's desk, his fists like rocks on the green blotter. He contemplated Taylor. He shifted his chewing gum to the other cheek. He smiled. "Who else wants a new principal?"

William and Bennie raised their hands. They lifted them slowly and kept their eyes on the floor.

"Well, I'm gonna tell you somethin," Robert said, sliding out from behind the desk. "You three is the only ones in here not doin any work. All you do is run off at the mouth."

Taylor and Bennie and William sat still. They stared at the floor.

"And I'll tell you what," Robert purred. "Any of you don't like the way I'm runnin things, you come do somethin about it." He prowled across the front of the room, massaging the knuckles of his right hand. The arena was empty. "All at once or one at a time."

Taylor and Bennie and William sat like statues. I was sitting at the back of the room.

"Come on!" The purr became a snarl. "You niggers

think you so bad, come on out and try to kick my ass."
Silence.

"You ain't shit, none of you. Now if all three of you ain't bad enough to come out here now, you keep your mouth shut and do what I say."

He dropped into the teacher's chair and propped his elbows on the blotter. "Now what else we got to take up at this meetin?"

Leonard paused in the doorway. His grin faded. He sniffed, as though he were trying to figure out the silence by its smell. The children sat rigid, their eyes riveted to their books. The tutors brooded. Robert had just thrown William into his chair and announced that the next tutor who took his eyes off his student was going to get hit "dead in his mouth." Leonard stepped forward tentatively, as though he were on thin ice. He was an elfish sixth grader.

"What you want, boy?" Robert barked.

"I'm waitin on William to tutor me," Leonard said.

"He's busy," Robert said.

"No I ain't," William piped up. He was surrounded by little girls.

"Didn't I tell you to work with them girls?" Robert bellowed.

William's eyes flickered, then fell again.

Robert's gaze crawled over the tutors. He spotted Sonny. "Sonny. Work with this boy."

Leonard looked at Sonny and wrinkled his nose as

though he had found an egg under the sofa three months after Easter. "I don't want to work with him."

"Shut up and get a book."

The children had stopped reading. Everyone was watching Leonard and Sonny.

Leonard put his hands in his pockets and strolled to the back of the room to the bookshelf. He scanned the rows, whistling softly. He chose a book and took it to Sonny. But Sonny had another book that he had picked up off the floor.

"Read this book," Sonny growled.

"I don't want to read that book." Leonard sat down beside Sonny.

"Read that book, boy." Sonny spit out the words.

Leonard looked at it as though Sonny had opened to the front page of *Little Women*. It was a fifth-grade reader. "I don't dig this book," Leonard said.

"Read that book or I'll smack you upside your head," Sonny croaked. He glanced at Robert. Robert presided with composed ferocity. "Tell him to read, Robert, or he gonna get hit," Sonny said.

Leonard put his head on the desk and covered himself with his hands.

Sonny looked at him, a badger and a rolled-up hedgehog. He tossed the book over his shoulder. It hit the window and fell open and twisted on the window ledge. "Fuck it," he said. He folded his arms. "Go read by your own damn self."

"Come here, boy." Robert's voice was like an axe breaking ice in the dawn.

Leonard stood up with the book he had chosen.

"I said come here."

Leonard walked a little more briskly over to Robert, carrying the book against his chest. It was called *Dogs*.

"Sit down, boy."

There was a chair next to Robert's. Leonard dragged it several feet away and sat down. Robert reached with his leg, hooked his foot around the chair leg, and yanked, nearly flipping Leonard off.

"Read."

Leonard opened the book. "The golden retriever gets its name from its long, golden coat. The golden retriever is a hunting dog."

Robert sat with his head cradled in his hands, watching his tutors. The children were reading again, their low garbled murmurs easing the silence. Robert's gaze shifted to Leonard. "Keep readin," he said.

Every morning the school served cereal, milk and juice on folding tables in the gym. One day when the kids were at breakfast, the principal walked in and found me alone.

"I'm looking for a boy in a striped shirt."

"What did he do?"

"He threw a rock at the milk truck."

"I'll find him," I said.

The gym was empty. The janitors were taking apart the portable tables. Some of my tutors were loitering in the hall.

"Get upstairs," I said.

"I thought Robert was in charge now."

"Just get upstairs."

They left the shadows along the wall. I headed for the door and ran into Robert, Sonny, Bennie and William. They had been out on Twelfth Street.

"Who threw the rock at the milk truck?" I said. Responsibility was dogging me.

"We been outside," Robert said coldly.

"So I see," I said.

They waited. I looked from shirt to shirt. Sonny's had red stripes.

"Looks as though it was you, Sonny," I said.

"So what if it was me?" Sonny's face was set, narrow-eyed, slack-jawed.

"So nothing," I said. "I have to try to keep you from getting fired." They looked at me as though it were my idea to fire Sonny. "Listen, will you all go on up to the room and stay there till I come back?" They started up.

The principal was in his office. An electric fan was spinning on the floor beside his desk. I told him that Sonny had thrown the rock. "If you'll let me talk to him, I think he'll settle down. He's been coming along beautifully."

The principal leaned back in his swivel chair and

smiled diffidently. "The boy should be thrown out. But I'll let you handle it your way."

"Thank you," I said.

A few days before, the math teacher had seen Sonny dragging a boy down the hall, cuffing him on the head. She had told the principal. At breakfast the principal had asked Sonny to carry some trash to the trash barrel twenty feet away. Sonny had refused.

I called him out of the room. "Look," I said. "Everything's straight now. Will you stay out of trouble?"

"Okay," Sonny said.

An hour later the tutors went out for a fifteen minute break. The principal motored in, his face lowered and red. "Sonny is out." His voice shook. His hands twitched. "If I catch him in the building again, I'm going to call the police."

He whirled and almost collided with Sonny on the threshold. "You," he quavered. "You're out. If I see you again, I'm going to call the police. That is final. Now I'll personally see you to the door."

"Shit, go ahead and call them," Sonny croaked. He followed the principal down the hall. Sandra was the only tutor in the room. There were six or seven children. I left them with her and went downstairs.

Sonny was leaning against the tree that grew through the sidewalk outside the school door. He stood as he used to in the doorways of the bars in the mornings when I passed him on my way to school. The elm cast a great pool of shade. The dust was white in the sun on the street. Several of the kids who worked for the janitor were sitting in the shade on the steps. I sat down with them.

"What happened, Sonny?" I said.

"We was runnin in the hall," Sonny grumbled. "Six of us runnin, and I'm the one he wants to fire. I'll kick his ass."

Robert burst out and landed on the sidewalk. "See?" he shrilled. "See? I knew I shouldn't have given you all no break. You play too much." He lit a cigarette and exhaled the blue smoke. "We got to talk it over with Davidson. Tell you what. We'll have a meetin. Right now."

Sonny leaned against the tree, staring across Twelfth Street.

"Come on, Mr. Hough." Robert hopped up the steps. "Come on, Sonny."

"I been throwed out, remember?" Sonny said. He sounded as though his name had just been dropped from the Social Register.

"Get your ass in here," Robert barked.

The tutors were all in the room. Robert sent the students home. "We got to decide," he began, "that we ain't gonna let no principal push us around." He met my eye. "You afraid of Davidson, Mr. Hough?" I was sitting at the back of the room.

"No, but I'm afraid of the police."

"The police ain't gonna do nothin," Robert said.

"I suggest you talk to Davidson," I said. "Ask him if Sonny can stay."

Just then the principal himself poked his head through the door. A hard silence met him. "John, may I speak to you?" He wanted to talk to me in his office.

"I just want to tell you a few things about your friend Sonny," he said. "I don't think you understand this boy." He recited Sonny's history. There were fights with teachers, smashed car windows, pulled fire alarms, thefts. Sonny had been to three junior high schools. Teachers couldn't reach him. He had been sent to a school for boys, a receptacle for kids who couldn't stop fighting the public school system.

"I knew all this when I hired him," I said.

The principal leaned forward and squeezed the edge of his desk. "I've given you *carte blanche* to do whatever you want. But you've hired the wrong students. You've hired young criminals. That's all they are. Young criminals."

"Yeah, but why?" I said. "Why are they criminals?"

"Listen." He leaned closer and squeezed harder. "This school is not a rehabilitation center. We don't have the time or resources to rehabilitate boys like Sonny. Ever since your thing began I've had complaints. Teachers have been complaining. Janitors have been complaining. Even the engineer has been complaining. I haven't passed on to you all the complaints."

It was true. We were both caught.

"Sonny Lamson is out. I can't have him in the building." He relaxed and leaned back. The chair squeaked. A secretary was hammering a typewriter. "You don't have the sociological training to deal with these boys," he said. "They need an expert."

Incompetence. I would have thought myself invulnerable to that word, too. The typewriter tapped erratic rhythms.

"By the way," the principal said. "Who broke my car window?"

"I can't tell you."

"Don't you trust me?" He sounded hurt.

"Sure. But I said I wouldn't tell." I stood up. The fan hurled its wind against my legs. "Would you come up and speak to them? They're having a meeting, and I think they'd like to talk to you."

"If you want." He peered through his plate-glass lenses. "Do you think it's a good idea?"

"A wonderful idea."

The room was quiet. I sat on the table at the back of the room. I felt as though I were sitting in the rear of a theater. The principal stayed close to the door.

He started with all the complaints that he had kept from us. "You're not students now," he said. "You're tutors, and in a way, you're members of the faculty. You have to obey the rules that the faculty obeys." It wasn't bad. Robert and Sonny studied their knuckles. The principal cleared his throat. "Does anyone have anything to say to me?" He waited a moment, then started to turn.

"I got somethin to say." It was Sonny.

"Yes?" The principal faced him from the doorway.

"Why is it you pick me out of six kids who was all runnin?"

"Frankly, it was because you were the one I saw. And because I had you on my mind, if you know what I mean."

"May I say somethin?" Robert. His voice was level, controlled. The principal folded his arms. "Sonny been doin his best work lately. I'm speakin for myself and the other tutors. We don't think Sonny should get fired."

"All right, Robert." The principal put his hands in his pockets. "I've cooled down. I'll go along with that."

"Thank you," Robert murmured.

The principal slid out and closed the door behind him. Everyone got up. They were like a team that has just won a big game.

"Mr. Hough," Sonny said. "If I hadn't of said nothin, he would of walked right out, ain't that right?"

"Sure he would have," I said.

They spilled out jubilantly and scattered across the parking lot. I crossed Twelfth Street with Robert and Sonny.

"You know something?" Robert said.

"What?"

"He ain't nothin to talk to."

We limped on, deeper and deeper into July. Like a painter who has mastered the artistic problems of his tableau, Robert lost interest. He relaxed. Someone lit a firecracker in the room. I was in the hall. I leaned on the door and stared at Robert. He smiled apologetically. Sonny punched Elaine in the mouth during breakfast one day. Elaine promised to come back with her brothers. Next day Sonny brought a piece of two-by-four to school. He and Robert fidgeted all day, up and down the stairs, spying nervously out the window. But no one came.

We lost students. They got tired of reading. They got tired of Robert and Sonny.

The first knot of panic came one evening at dusk. It stirred somewhere deep down and wriggled up into my stomach. I could feel it there, like a twitching bird. I needed faces. I needed laughter. I sat down on the rickety double bed. The smoky evening breeze sifted in through the torn screen. My silent distress signals spread and were lost in endless smog.

My record player crouched in its dusty corner. I chose a stack of records and lay on the bed and stared at the mustard-colored ceiling. *An American in Paris*. A sidewalk café, a glass of dry vermouth. The women clicking past on spike heels, so beautiful and so chic. Beethoven's Sixth Symphony. A June morning on the island. The sun on the tall grass, the sun on the moss and the silver-gray stone walls. Schubert's "Unfinished." Christmas. The smells of evergreen and tangerines. A fire on the hearth. *Chuck Berry's Golden Decade*. I was very young then, and the railroad still ran past our house. You could climb the apple tree and eat sour apples and watch the five-thirty from Boston, so far out on a limb that you could feel the rush of air as the train howled past.

The breeze died and the half-light deepened. The silence was empty and terrifying. I turned the records over. I was asleep before the silence returned. Sometime around two it rained. The patter swelled, and furious drops pounded the garbage cans in the alley. Then the rain receded, farther and farther and farther away, and I was asleep again.

Richard Cross had once been a minister. He was an earnest young man with curly yellow hair and rimless glasses. He had worked with migrant farmers in Appalachia. Now he was the Vista Field Analyst in Detroit. I went to see him. We had coffee around the corner from the Federal Building.

"I've got to go home," I said. People streamed past on the sidewalk. This was the land of swept sidewalks and wall-to-wall carpets.

Dick Cross studied me. "I think you do," he said.

"I won't pull out till summer school is over," I said. That would be the end of July. I was supposed to leave Vista at the end of August. "If the school program lasted longer, I'd stay longer. But it's ending, and I got to get out of here."

"Don't worry about it," he said. "You've done fine.

There wouldn't be much you could do anyway. It would be too late to start a new program."

"I shouldn't leave," I said.

"Don't worry about it," he said again. We got up. He paid for the coffee and we walked out into the glare. "You might even want to come back into Vista," Dick said. "Think about it. After you've got yourself together at home."

"Sure," I said.

We parted at the white stone steps of the Federal Building. "Let me know before you leave," he said.

"I'm sorry," I said.

"Forget it."

ELEVEN

ONE DAY near the end the school showed a movie in the auditorium. We sent all our children. There weren't many now. Sandra's little girls and a rugged core of six or seven boys were all that remained. It was another blistering day, white-hot sun and white dust in the streets. We left the children in the auditorium and went out and sat in the shade on the steps. No one said anything. A new wing was being built at the end of the school. We lounged on the steps, and the only sound was the grinding of the crane and an occasional shout by one of the construction workers.

Sonny struck a match on the cement and lighted a cigarette. He was leaning against the wall, drawing silently, when the principal walked out. The principal had to step over me and Bennie. He spotted Sonny's cigarette.

"John, what's this boy doing smoking at the door?" He had had almost all he could take. I felt sorry for him. His job was here and he had to stick with it. His impossible job.

"Boy?" Sonny put his hands on his hips and cocked his head.

The principal ignored him. "It never ends, it never ends," he muttered.

"Sonny," I said softly. "Put it out, will you?"

Sonny watched the principal cross the street to his car, then took a last drag and dropped the cigarette on the pavement. It was less than half smoked.

"Thanks," I said.

We sat there, listening to the rumble of the crane. The construction company had gouged out part of a lot that had been cleared next to the school. Timbers, concrete blocks, and bricks littered the baked dirt.

Suddenly Bennie jumped up off the step. "Hey, Mr. Hough." His eyes sparkled. "Get me one of them bricks, William." He bit a smile. "Listen, Mr. Hough. I can break a brick with my bare hand."

"Sure," I said.

Robert stared gloomily out toward Twelfth Street. Sonny cleaned his fingernails with his knife. No one except William paid attention. William headed for the construction site and came back lugging a cinder block at his belt. It was two inches thick, a coarse gray block like a slab of concrete. William set it on the sidewalk at my feet.

"I can break that with my bare hand," Bennie said.

I examined it. It was heavy and as hard as brick. "Sure you can," I said.

"Bet," Bennie said.

"How much?"

"Fifty cents."

"All right."

Robert blinked at the cinder block. Sonny folded his knife.

William scurried away and came back with two more cinder blocks. He set them on end on the sidewalk, then laid the third block across the top, like the top of a table. Robert heaved himself off the wall and came over and stood above the blocks. The others circled Bennie. William stepped aside and Bennie knelt in front of the altar of cinder blocks. He flattened his hand and stroked it tenderly. He flashed a smile at the audience. Then he raised his arm and, with a short, sharp chop, hacked the cinder block in two.

He jumped up and William slapped his palms. I paid him.

"Get me one of them blocks," Robert roared.

William scampered to the gutted lot and staggered back loaded with three more blocks. They must have cost thirty-five cents apiece. I don't know how William picked them up with the workers all over. He set up a block for Robert. Robert knelt, frowning. He studied the block. He studied his hand. He split the cinder block with a vicious snap.

"How'd you like him to hit you on your mouth with that hand?" Sonny chattered.

William set up another. "Mr. Hough, you got to try it." They all shouted at me. I knelt by the block and hit it as hard as I could. It broke, all right.

"Say," I said. "Maybe we can make some money with this."

They all looked at me.

"Hide the busted pieces," I said. They pounced on the jagged halves and hurled them around the corner of the building. We sat down on the steps. Five minutes later Mrs. Davis, the community agent, came out.

"Hey, Mrs. Davis." I jumped up, blocking her way. "Look at this block." I picked it up and held it so she could examine it. "I bet you fifty cents Bennie can break it with his bare hand."

She felt the block. "What you talkin about?"

"I'll bet you fifty cents." The kids watched the traffic on Twelfth Street.

"Then you got a trick," Mrs. Davis said.

"Look." I rotated the block slowly.

"With his bare hand?" she said.

"Sure."

"I'll bet you a quarter," she said.

William set up the block and Bennie ambled over and lopped it in two. The kids exploded, bouncing up off the steps and holding their sides. Mrs. Davis found a quarter in her purse.

"I'll give you the next one," I told Bennie.

Pretty soon Miss Singer came out. She was a secretary, a black girl. She was lean and voluptuously feline. She picked her way down the steps among the kids, and I got up and did my act. Miss Singer examined the block.

"What you up to?" she said. She had long eyelashes. The kids snickered.

"Nothing but a quarter bet," I said.

She looked at Bennie. *"He* gonna break this brick?" We all laughed. She took the bet.

After she had paid, we watched her cross the street. She wore a tight sweater and a tight skirt.

"You should of bet her for her phone number, Mr. Hough," William said. We laughed.

Sonny cackled like a mirthful chimpanzee. "Shit, you should of bet her more than that."

The movie ended. The children poured out of the seams of the school. It was almost noon. "Let's call it a day," I said.

"Want me to go up to the room and dismiss everybody?" Sonny offered.

"That would be real nice of you," I said. He got up and scooted into the school. We sat on the steps until the last bell rang and the school emptied. I could have sat there all afternoon.

"You been a good tenant," Mr. Hunter said, chewing his cigar.

I remembered the hard stare he had thrown at me that day last September, the eyes like an owl's behind the glasses.

"Yes sir, you ain't been no trouble. I sure am sorry to see you go."

Well, I had paid on time and I had been quiet.

"You've been all right yourself," I said. We shook hands. "Don't work too hard."

He took the cigar out of his mouth and lowered his voice. "If somethin don't happen soon, I'm gettin out of this buildin. Fella that owns it, rich Jewish fella, I offered him cash money for it. But he don't want to sell."

I had assumed all along that Mr. Hunter owned the building. But it was another piece of white-owned property.

"Let him run it his own damn self," Mr. Hunter was saying.

"That's right," I said.

"If you ever get back this way," he said, "stop and see us." He stood in the dark hall, short and blurred.

"I sure will," I said.

He was gone.

That night my windows were open as usual to the smells and noises of the alley. Some kids passed, talking loudly. Their footsteps crunched on the gravel and broken glass, and their voices faded like an engine in a tunnel. Out on Hamilton the drone of traffic was punctuated by the shriek of rubber skidding on asphalt. Now and then an explosion popped somewhere. Was it a gun or a firecracker? I never learned to distinguish the sounds. It was a night like any other.

The sun didn't ease up for my last day. I perspired as I walked to school. The sky was blue and cloudless. Whiskey bottles, emptied the night before, lay still unbroken in the doorways to the upstairs apartments. An abandoned car, its wheels stripped, wallowed at the curb. The windshield was a field of silver splinters. The taillights were smashed. A Tactical Mobile Unit car prowled past. The panel on the top of the Sears Building flashed time and temperature in the eternal rhythm of the city. It was all just as it had been last September. It was just as it had been before I got there.

A few of the tutors were sitting on the steps. I joined them. Robert and Sonny sauntered up. They said hello and went in. Five minutes later they came back. They held a carton of milk in each hand. The principal was yapping at their heels. "If you want milk, why don't you ask for it?" They walked away from him, carrying the milk. He stopped on the top step. They leaned against a car. He looked at them as though he had been trying since they were babies to teach them to say excuse me after they burped. Robert and Sonny set the cartons of milk on the car roof and folded their arms.

"What happened?" I said.

It was the principal's last chance. He took it. "It's you," he shouted. "It's your fault. It's all been your fault." His cheeks were pink. "You brought these boys into the school and turned them loose. You can't control them. It's been your fault from the beginning."

I just sat there. I was going home.

"It ain't your fault, Mr. Hough." It was Robert. He stood on spread, planted legs and squinted into the sun. "It ain't your fault."

"Of course it's my fault," I said.

"No, it ain't your fault," Robert said.

"They'll put the milk back," I told the principal.

"It's not that," he said. "We have plenty of milk. If they would only ask."

The engineer trudged up out of the furnace room. He wore olive-green shirt and pants, streaked with soot and grime. His face was smudged. His hands were black. "Listen," I said. "Now that it's over I want to apologize for the trouble my boys gave you." He had run into Robert and Sonny in the basement several times.

"Don't worry about it," he said.

"No," I said, "I brought these kids into the school and inflicted them on everyone else. It really wasn't fair."

"Don't worry about it."

"It was just an idea I had," I said.

"What was?"

"Bringing in those kids."

He lit a cigarette. His slicked-down hair looked like varnished straw. "You got to try," he said.

"It was just an idea." They were going to spend five hours a day teaching little children to read. They were going to be good to the children.

"Some idea," I said.

Robert was waiting on Twelfth Street. I stopped on the corner. We stood there alone in the quiet afternoon.

"You really goin?" he said.

"I have to."

"I didn't think you was goin so soon."

"Well . . ."

"When you comin back?"

"I don't know."

"Man, why don't you work here next year?"

"I don't have a job here."

He lit a cigarette. "You know you could get a job here if you wanted to." He examined his cigarette.

"I just have to go for a while," I said.

"I won't be seein you then." He said it as though it had just come to him.

"I'll write to you," I said. "I promise."

I stuck out my hand and we shook. His hand was hard and calloused. He turned to cross Twelfth Street, rolling slowly, like a tired sailor.

The jet gathered speed and vaulted off the runway. Detroit became a meadow spangled with thousands of tiny lights, tilting and whirling and then getting smaller. We punched up into the clouds and emerged into the silent world above. The western sky blazed. You could barely hear the engines. I had been airlifted out of the wire and asphalt.

In Boston the salty night air pressed in off the bay and draped the airfield. It was a smell of summer, a smell of home. My mother and sister met me. I knew they would both be there.

Our headlights cut the foggy, salty darkness as we

sped down Route 3. There would be people to see now. Holding their drinks, they would stand on a porch facing Vineyard Sound or a lawn above Quissett Harbor. Their legs and necks would be brown, and they would be wearing Bermuda shorts and laundered sneakers. Of course they would know what Vista was; and they would ask me about my experiences. I would try to tell them. They would keep interrupting me, enthusiastically. "I don't know how you did it."

I would tell them that I did nothing. I would tell them that I changed nothing.

"You did more than you think," they would say affectionately. "You did plenty." Then they would smile past me at my parents and, sipping our drinks, we would all turn to watch the sun set behind the harbor.

My brother helped me drag my luggage across the lawn. My father shook my hand warmly, silently. The crickets chirped somewhere in the pine trees. I smelled the honeysuckle. The stars sparkled and the sky was hard and slick, as though someone had wiped away the smudge with a rag dipped in alcohol.

My room smelled sweet and musty. I would have to look for the books my sisters always borrowed when I was away. I noticed the Hornblower books were missing. This time I would have to check my brother's room too.

It is many months later, many parties later. The parties are inside now, around pine fires and punchbowls.

"I don't know how you did it," they say, as I knew they would.

"You'll never regret it," they declare. Even those who hear me out insist that it was an honorable failure.

Maybe it was. But I still didn't understand the year, not until I recalled what the school engineer told me the last day. "You got to try," he said. And I had. Stories have morals where I grew up, and to try is honorable.

I don't know why the kids had tried. There was so little to try for. But the engineer must have been right.